ΛPPALΛCHIΛN
HERITAGE

VOL. 47, NO. 2
SPRING 2019

EDITOR
Jason Howard

STUDENT ASSISTANTS
Frankie Baldwin, Rhea Carter & Emily Masters

MANUSCRIPT READERS
Katherine Scott Crawford & Patti Frye Meredith

ESTABLISHED IN 1973

PUBLISHED QUARTERLY
by Berea College
CPO 2166
205 N. Main Street
Berea, KY, 40404

www.appalachianheritage.net

The short stories in this publication are works of fiction. Names, characters, places, and incidents are either the products of the authors' imaginations or are used fictitiously. Any resemblance to actual events, locales, or persons, living or dead, is entirely coincidental. The views expressed in the creative nonfiction herein are solely those of the authors.

Electronic submissions only at www.appalachianheritage.net

Distributed by the University of North Carolina Press. Basic subscription price: $30/year for individuals, $40/year for institutions. For subscription requests and inquiries, visit the magazine's website, email uncpress_journals@unc.edu, or call 919.962.4201.

CONTENTS

INTERVIEW

CRAFT ESSAY

BOOK REVIEWS

EDITOR'S NOTE

JASON HOWARD

Two months ago I turned to my husband with a prophecy: "This, for me, is about to be a season of lessons."

I am not an oracle—the signs were simply inscribed everywhere I turned. After a year of prevaricating, we have embarked upon a move following nearly ten years spent in an old Craftsman-style home we deeply loved. What's more, the health of our beloved sixteen-year-old dachshund was becoming increasingly precarious. He had gone into kidney failure, and while a stint in hospital had helped him to rebound for the time being, I worried he would leave this world while I was teaching a study abroad course for three weeks in Ireland.

These twin transitions had stirred up intense emotions in me. While we both needed a change in geographic location, I was grieving all the living, loving, writing, and reading we had done in our home, and how often that had been connected to our eldest dog. It felt like I was bidding a long goodbye to both home and companion.

But there was more—a bedrock of sadness, a hard truth about my life I needed to confront. I had become too busy. Over the past several years, I had grown accustomed to saying yes to everything that came my way—to every reading, course, workshop, conference, writing assignment, and responsibility that presented itself, and I was now left to wonder where the time had gone.

Two years away from forty, I realized the necessity of reconstructing my life around quality rather than quantity. I wanted more time for writing, for books and music, for dogs, for family.

Literature, like life, also comes with lessons, and this issue of *Appalachian Heritage* is not exception. There are hard-won revelations nestled in these stories, essays, and poems, and if you listen while you read, they will make themselves known— quietly, in a whisper that brushes your earlobe. "Remember who you are," a father reminds his daughter in "The Dance" by beloved Appalachia author George Ella Lyon. This excerpt from a novel-in-progress anchors a special fiction section, one featuring the voices of young female narrators in stories by Cathy Cruise, Bre Lillie, and Kim Shegog.

The value of friendship forged by a shared love of nature is celebrated and memorialized in Catharina Coenen's exquisite, probing essay "Invasive," and the natural world is commemorated in verse by poets including Jeff Worley, Llewellyn McKernan, Kathleen Brewin Lewis, Noah Davis, and M.S. Reagan. Award-winning poet and teacher Marianne Worthington provides insighful tips about submitting work to literary magazines, while Jessica Chiccehitto Hindman discusses her newly published and acclaimed memoir *Sounds Like Titanic.* Our reviews section considers the merits of two recently published works: *WWJD and Other Poems* by Savannah Sipple and *The Sound of Holding Your Breath* by Natalie Sypolt.

For now, I have committed myself to a slower pace, one I will strive to maintain over the summer and beyond, placing places a premium on deeper experiences with family, friends, and art—and listening. ∎

THE DANCE
(1939)

GEORGE ELLA LYON

1

Mickey had just buttoned the last button of her navy blue polka-dot dress when her brother Ben hollered from the hall. "Aren't you too little to be going to a dance?"

"Oh, shush," she said, coming out of the bedroom and giving him a playful push on the shoulder. She had to reach up to do it, and it didn't move in the least. "You're not the only one growing up," she said. "I won't be your kid sister forever."

"Yes, you will," he told her. "And I'm grown, not growing. Out in the big world earning my way. You're not even fifteen."

"In December I will be," Mickey said, starting downstairs. Ben followed. On the sill of the window where the staircase turned, late-summer light caught the ruby rim of the bowl their mother kept there.

■ ■ ■

Born in 1924, the fourth child and third daughter in the Bruton brood, Mickey had settled easily into the life of this big family which until three years ago, was always moving from one mountain settlement to another, wherever her dad could be hired to cut and finish a boundary of timber. Mickey was too little to notice how the Depression pushed them into smaller and smaller houses, how it thinned the milk gravy and lined her father's face. It sharpened her mother's tongue, too, but Mickey didn't feel the slice of that. Her oldest sister Glynis mostly raised her.

With Ben, Glynis and Eva all older than she was, Mickey felt sheltered wherever they lived. There were always arms to pick her up or a lap to sit in. Times were hard, but they weren't hard for her.

Goose Rock, Manchester, Pikeville, Virgie—these were the little coal towns in Kentucky where Mickey remembered living. With this last move, three years ago, Dave Bruton had had the means to build a good-sized sawmill, and business was booming. The mines were working three shifts and constantly needed timbers to support the roofs and lumber for company houses. *Their* house on Cedar Street was a two-story bungalow with three bedrooms, a dining room big enough to seat them all, and a kitchen where Ruby Bruton said she finally had space to cook and breathe at the same time.

■ ■ ■

Eva, the sister between her and Glynis, had just finished the dishes when Mickey came downstairs. Their mother was resting in her bedroom just off the living room, and their dad, still in khaki work clothes, was on the front porch with his pipe and the newspaper.

"You need earbobs," Eva said. "White, to set off the dots."

"I don't have any."

"You can wear mine," Eva said.

"Whit will be here any minute," Mickey told her.

"Hold on," Eva insisted, moving past her and running up the stairs.

Mickey stepped out on the porch to watch for Whit. Her dad looked up from the news.

"I'm afraid you're growing up on me," he said.

"Oh, Daddy." Mickey ran her hands down the sides of her skirt.

"Here!" Eva huffed, coming through the screen door. She held out her hand where white earbobs nested like eggs. Mickey lifted them out, one at a time, and put them on.

"Ouch! They pinch!"

"Baby!" Eva taunted. "They make you look more put together, even wearing Glynis's old dress."

"I love this dress," Mickey said.

Aroogha, Aroogha! Whit had arrived.

"Does that boy not have the decency—" Mickey's dad began, but then he saw Whit Daniels striding up the walk.

When Whit saw Mickey, willowy in her navy dress, her dark curly hair pulled away from her face, he gave a wolf whistle before he saw Mr. Bruton, scowling up at him.

"Sorry, sir," he said. "She, uh, your daughter, well, *Mickey*, looks so good all dressed up."

Dave Bruton stood. Whit held out his hand. They shook.

"You're Tom's boy?" Whit nodded. "Behave yourself," he said, and Whit nodded again. "Have her back by ten,"

"Yes, sir," Whit promised and offered his hand to Mickey.

This wasn't a date. Mickey wasn't allowed to date yet. His dad's car was full of a big gang of his friends and the Suzy-Q girls who were putting on the dance. But because her dad and her sisters were watching, and because she was tired of forever being the kid, she took it.

"Remember who you are," her dad told her. Mickey went on tiptoes and kissed him on the cheek.

Halfway down the walk she slid the earbobs off and put them in her purse.

2

It is just that way sometimes. It was just that way. Cliffs do not care, cars do not care, whiskey sure as hell doesn't care. It just happens that a boy's head goes light and his foot goes heavy and squeals of joy turn inside out as the wheel spins useless in his hands.

If Whit's daddy hadn't been a car dealer, so proud of next-year's Olds with its Hydramatic transmission, and Whit had had to shift gears. If Tom Daniels had done what he intended and made Whit drive the old Buick. If Janet had never had the idea to put on a beginning-of-school dance. If Anna and Lizzie had never dreamed up the Suzy-Qs. If there had been one fewer passenger in the car.

Everyone was pretty well wedged in the Olds except the funniest, the prettiest, the Mickeyest. She was sitting on Lizzie's lap in the front seat. She had her head just a little out the window, breathing the deep leafiness of August threaded with the mineral tang of creek water singing down the mountain.

It had rained earlier in the day and the blacktop was steamy and maybe still just a little bit slick. It happens like that.

This wasn't on the way to the dance, held at the country club because Anna's family owned a coal mine so they could afford the fee. It was at intermission, when the kids were all het up from dancing and high spirits.

"Let's go for a ride," Whit said, and the Suzy-Q's and their would-be dates climbed in the car docile as babies. Girls first. The guys had to suck on their bottles.

Minutes later Mickey was thrown out the window, almost as if the cliff wanted her, pulled her. We know that isn't true. Nevertheless she flew straight to its limestone breast. None of the other kids were really hurt.

And Mickey wasn't hurt. She was killed. ■

NAMESAKE

This name came to me from the Smokies,
the foothills, the footsteps of my fathers
who walked the farm with the tobacco
jungles where I once disappeared

as a child, absorbed into groping green
curtains of sticky hands broad and veinous.
Sprinting wild, my feet thunder,
thumping on paths of burnt umber,
I raced against myself to shake loose
this name— what it signified—
only to emerge with a clammy headache,
sick with the fever of July.

Instead this name became the chigger
that burrowed into my thigh that day,
becoming as much my flesh as a freckle,
a parasitic ember I tried to quench
with fingernails until skin pinked raw.

Each September it became the ghost
of that chigger, haunting my ears in blush
and burn when the teacher read this name
from the roster. Classmates laughed
because everyone knew me as my middle;
only my mother invoked this name
when I was in the deepest of trouble.

This name still inhabits my blood
the way this sex is a leech between my legs,
this need to scratch them both out—
something fierce.

IV.

This name is really my father's, his daily driver,
his inheritance from the farm, where as a child
he beheld fruit and nuts in bushel baskets,
simple Christmas gifts from his grandfather.

Where as a teen he carved this name
plus my mother's with a pocketknife
into the wall of the pitch pine smokehouse.

This name a threaded sheen of white script
embroidered onto his blue work uniform,
blotched with grease from diesel engines,
scarecrowed on the clothesline.

When he came home I saw the cost
of using hands to put food on the table:
thin black tattoos of grease staining crevices,
chunked knuckles adorned with ruby scabs,
sometimes a swollen inkwell of blood
pressurizing beneath the smashed thumbnail—
a 1/64th inch hole drilled for relief. Once he
came home crowned with a crescent moon
gouge on his scalp.

He engraved the initial of this name
in wobbled cursive onto the wrenches
and sockets I was made to fetch

as a youth in his cold garage, where he
could fix anything except his temper.

The M. stood at times for *malodorous mood*,
at times for *mellow*, for *motorcycle*, for *mechanic*,
for *masculinity*: something foreign to me as a sea
on the planet Mars. The M. was most certainly
not a stand in for *mother's make-up*—
what I applied to my face when home alone.

Yet once, my mother screamed this name
one night when my little sister suffered
another grand mal seizure, and I awoke
yelling *What?!* into the darkness.

III.

My grandfather, who grew up barefoot
on the farm using his middle name too,
has an eighth grade education, but knows
how to harvest tobacco, cure a pig with salt,
catch snapping turtles by the sackful,
hunt and fish, but had this name,
his first name, stamped onto his dog tags
during the Korean War while stationed
in Pittsburgh. He stayed to work as a machinist,
crossed the Allegheny in his Chevrolet,
atop the arches of the 40th Street Bridge
to mill cold steel at Heppenstall, used this name
on his timecard, became this name,
along with a self-taught carpenter, plumber,
electrician, mason, small engine mechanic,
architect, and contractor, who with my
teenage father's help, built his own

two-story home in the suburbs—
which I continue to visit each Christmas.

I grew up believing he worked as a barber—
sat on an old barbershop chair in his garage
silently mourning each little silken clump
that fell onto the cape. Grew up with a secret
desire for long hair, fearful of the wide leather
razor strap he sometimes snapped— playfully—
but afraid because he once got chigger-faced,
at a family reunion, quoting a bible verse
after he mistook a longhaired nephew for a girl.

My grandfather with this name that I share,
who can type and is computer literate,
once told me in his Tennessee tongue—
still slow after all of these years—
once told me his secret: he simply believed
he could achieve anything he put his mind to.

What I wanted to say but didn't was: *grandpa,*
sometimes my mind is too much a tornado
to put towards anything, let alone believe
in myself, besides, what I really want is a secret
you'll never hear me speak, because I'm afraid
of losing you, even though we share this name.

After estrogen, after growing out my hair,
I'm still afraid, even though he sometimes jokes:
Come visit me anytime, just don't show-up
at my door wearing lipstick, or else
I'm liable not to recognize you.

II.

This name came to my grandpa from his father,
the farmer who drove a horse drawn cart
from the dusty lanes lined with tobacco
to Knoxville where he sold his crops at market—
a two day affair, who lived his whole life
without indoor plumbing, until he came in
from the field one day and fell down.
This man I've never met, my great-grandfather,
who they say was a good man,
cared for his mother until her death,
climbed the foothills with his wife
to pick huckleberries that sold in Maryville,
where he was known to sell them in cups not level
but heaping, to black and white folks alike.
This name I share with him as well,
wonder if I will be made to rest in its gender,
under its weight engraved in granite.

I.

M. is also for *mystery*, there was one other
of this name, one shrouded in the mountain
mists of my grandpa's childhood memory—
one existing in his grandmother's cryptographs,
a grandfather spoken of only when her story
demanded a bookmark, a this was *before
I stayed with him.*

I clicked through an online genealogy,
exhumed his skeleton in HTML:
great-great grandfather was not married to her,
but rather to her sister, and for a time
they all lived together. I closed the window,

kept her secret safe alongside mine,
safe for the sake of my namesakes.

■ ■ ■

Through this name I'm yoked to stout
Scots-Irish necks—generations
of firstborn males baptizing me
into a field of mud, where I've plowed
myself in circles, nearly into The Pit—
abode of the dead, whose throngs
sometimes brush my shoulders,
whose songs sometimes whisper
in the obscurest planes of my mind.

This name. This sex. This M.
This lifetime of tectonics:
efface and become, colliding.
Call me mountain.

Crop of tobacco smoked. Stalks uprooted.
In this fallow field I'll grow marigolds,
I'll run between their rows.

M.S. REAGAN

THE LAST WILD PASSENGER PIGEON MAKES HER CONCESSION SPEECH

My mother called me *Piqua*, as she bent
over our warm whorl with bits of worm.

A word she taught me: *flock*.
How I dreamt of them, a feathered rising
above the trees, cries of *coo-roo coo-roo*.
Safety in numbers, winged joy!

They hunted us, devoured us.
One day we were gone. I combed
the woods for markings like mine:
blue-gray head, rosy breast, graceful neck.
I called into the deep hush.

I have lost the race.

KATHLEEN BREWIN LEWIS

AFTER THE BLIGHT

after Anya Silver

The poem was the wood and the way out of the wood.
The poet wound her way through a forest,
up to the porch of an old cabin, its floor planked
with chestnut cut and planed before the blight,
back when the trees cast shady alcoves,
sheltered songbirds. (Remember the smell
of roasting chestnuts?) She napped on the porch,
on the smooth planks, rose to gather fresh words,
plucked them from the limbs of the ghost trees,
lined up the words, sent the poem downstream,
out of the wood and into the field,
which was full of light.

KATHLEEN BREWIN LEWIS

INVASIVE

CATHARINA COENEN

What are these?" Judy asks. She bends way down, peers over the gold rims of her spectacles at something green beside the path. My eyes dash away from her, scan patch snow between silver trunks of beech and birch to find the dogs, team-digging for chipmunks by a stump. Clots of soil and rock are hitting leaf-duff in rhythmic spurts. They'll be busy for awhile.

I crouch next to Judy for a closer look. Tiny white flowers, about a dozen in a bunch, a fairy bridal bouquet ascending from a rosette of heart-shaped leaves. Some smaller leaves wind in a spiral staircase up the flower-bearing stem. I hook my glasses into my sweater collar, get down on hands and knees, bring my good right eye in close: four petals, six stamens.

"Some mustardy thing."

I need to bring the little flowers home to reference books and tea to extend my diagnosis beyond family resemblance, pin down a species name—but I won't pick them if there are just a few. Unfolding my achy back and dampish knees, I put my glasses on, then look around. There are four. No, five. I know I've never seen them here; but still, those tooth-edged leaves do resonate—familiar shapes I cannot place. Judy has been walking dogs along these trails since before blueberry bogs succumbed to soccer fields. If she thinks these rosettes of saw-toothed hearts are new arrivals to these woods, then they are new. For now, I'll have to leave them be.

The dogs dig deeper, taking turns at the same hole. Judy and I return to talk of flowers waking from their winter's nap—this morning, the clump of bloodroot we transplanted from her yard to mine sent up first leaves, furled like umbrellas as they push from softening ground; soon it will be time to look for blue *Hepatica*.

Since we've started talking botany on daily walks, what I am planting in my garden has become a subject of earnest inquiry, as have my curtains, my cutlery, my compost pile, the health of my family in Germany, and anything I've ever cooked. Swept up in shared bouts of farmer's market shopping, canning, and impromptu barbecues, I've stopped wondering how long teaching college biology can keep me happy on the northern edge of Appalachia, three thousand miles from home.

Today, the chipmunks' burrow proves too deep for digging dogs. Judy and I pick up our pace, take the shortcut across the parking lot between the college football and baseball fields; Judy mustn't be late for her doctor's appointment.

"Call me when you get back," I say.

Her symptoms, reported over many weeks, have puzzled me—evening chills and fevers that resolve by morning, a pain she describes as "a stitch in my side."

"Or, I can tell you tomorrow," Judy says.

■ ■ ■

The dogs have treed a squirrel. Two weeks have transformed fairy bridal bouquets into candelabras by our path. Like dollhouse-cucumbers, green fruits curve skyward from stems that have shot up knee-high. Two neat seams that split the oldest fruits signify siliques—another mustard hallmark.

Judy's scans are back. "Diverticulitis," the doctor said, a small pouch on the colon that swells and gets infected off and on, not too unusual in late middle-age. Some intravenous antibiotics should calm the ooze and swelling, clear things up. The squirrel jumps, catches another branch; dogs rage below to no avail. There's a squirrel highway in this canopy, and each nodding twig asserts escape.

■ ■ ■

My dog's high-pitched yelps, hot on a rabbit's brushy tracks, lead me away from our familiar round of trails. Summer-green privet covers the mad zigzag of his dash and Judy cannot help me look. After four weeks of fevers and recurring pains her doctors, out of drugs to try, went radical; a surgery has clipped that oozing pouch—she should come home in just another week. I follow fading yelps and rustles down an unfamiliar trail, then stop to listen, scan for movement between oak and brush. I whistle, listen, whistle, wait.

Rangy green candelabras frame this path. Where fruits gape open, black seeds glint in single rows. Yet, at the apex of each shoot, more flower buds announce: These plants intend to go on blooming. Diminishing this fertile bunch by just one will do no harm—I pick a specimen to take it home to books and tea, then drop it as a cloud of garlic rises from bruised leaves. My nose knows before there are words or names: This is the smell of straying from a European woodland path, the taste of springtime omelets. *Alliaria*, a genus name reeking of onions. The truth of its relations to the Allium family, however, the leeks and garlics, onions and chives, lies not in genes or marriage, just in pungency.

Garlic mustard—a name to drop by Judy's bed this afternoon; woodland news and speculations, a green gossip column to walk her mind away from drips of the IV. The doctors sent some tissues out for biopsy; no need to worry, just routine. The rabbit's gone to ground, my dog is back, trailing broken brambles: prickles of blackberry, hooked thorns of multiflora rose.

■ ■ ■

Siliques on tall stems rustle, parched and ripe in their mid-summer tan. Seeds scatter as dogs fling themselves from the trail, traversing weeds to reach the brush. After a grouse? A turkey? From sprays of *Rosa multiflora* quivering in their wake, I turn to Judy, dumbly repeat words, like new vocabulary in a language class:

"Stage IIIB."

Blood pounds in my ears.

"I'll call you when I've looked it up."

"Tell me tomorrow," Judy says. "There's nothing to decide today."

Whatever the dogs scared up has flown; my lanky setter-mix returns, then Ivy, Judy's terrier, short-legged in his wake. Flanks pump, pink tongues loll from wide-open jaws. They trail us, slowly, panting hard, as we extend a walk devoid of words, humid heat plastering our shirts against our backs.

An hour later, I lift my tea cup, realize it's empty. I've been meaning to make more. An asterisk in *Newcomb's Wildflower Guide*—means alien, correct? Correct: "The plant is not native to the area but has been brought in by one means or another."

Newcomb's and I have always got along.

"Brought in from where?"

Newcomb's is silent on this point.

"Native to Europe," *The Flora of Pennsylvania* says.

My nose was right: Garlic mustard smells of childhood romps.

"So, how did it get here?"

Google, ever solicitous, suggests the National Park Service for further inquiries. There, the Alien Plants Working Group speculates that settlers brought garlic mustard along with them for food or maybe medicine. A first record from 1868 pins it to Long Island, a rural get-away for summering city folks.

Brought here to work, then, and escaped. From fields and gardens seeds scattered to the woods—feral white flowers tracing the white man's path across a continent, making themselves at home in patchy sunlight under disturbed deciduous canopies.

Now that it's in our woods and free to run along cross-country trails, what will it do? On this point, the Alien Plants Working Group sounds definite: "Once introduced to an area, garlic mustard outcompetes native plants by aggressively monopolizing light, moisture, nutrients, soil and space."

Aggressively monopolizing space.

I lift my cup. There is no tea. I put the cup down on the table, then my arms and head.

Google, infamous for side-tracked conversations, always makes me ask more questions than I opened the computer for. How did my fingers jump from mustards to Stage IIIB? The answer is forty-six percent. One in two people die within five years. Have the doctors really not told her this?

I lift my face. My eyes touch the phone, recoil, then seek safety on the computer screen. "A single plant can produce thousands of seeds, which scatter as much as several meters from the parent plant." Scatter how far?

I get up, fill the kettle, then walk up and down the stairs. Scatter to kidneys, liver, spine?

Water and metal grumble, pop; the kettle heats.

What was I wanting from upstairs? Another book?

How did my fingers jump from mustards to Stage IIIB? The answer is forty-six perecent. One in two people die within five years. Have the doctors really not told her this?

I walk back down, plop back onto my chair. "Recognition of garlic mustard is critical. Several white-flowered native plants, including toothworts (*Dentaria*), sweet cicely (*Osmorhiza claytonii*), and early saxifrage (*Saxifraga virginiensis*), occur alongside garlic mustard and may be mistaken for it."

To see garlic mustard, you must train your eye to find four petals, heart-shaped leaves, fruits splitting along two seams— the patterns that distinguish natives from invaders.

My teeth have peeled a strip of skin from my lower lip. The blood tastes metallic, familiar. I dab. That surgeon had no idea he was dealing with cancer when he sliced the diverticulum away from Judy's gut. He said he saw nothing suspicious there at all.

The kettle whistles, I jump up, turn off the gas, sit back down. "Care must be taken to remove the plant with its entire root system because new plants can sprout from root fragments." Next to the computer sits a Kleenex, with some dots of blood.

Recognition is critical. And now the surgeon says he "thinks" he's "got it all."

I pick up the phone.

"Go down to the university medical center," I say. "Get in on their drug trial, if that's the only way your insurance will let you go."

Judy says Laura, her sister, has already told her this.

I say: "I'm glad."

I say: "Please go."

I reach for my tea cup. There is nothing in it.

"I'll tell you tomorrow," Judy says.

■ ■ ■

Snow devils dance across the soccer fields. My dog leaves impact craters as he bounds. Behind him, Judy's terrier plows slow furrows, pushing snow. I turn around to Judy in my tracks: "You sure you want to do this?"

Her glasses fog below the thick brim of her hat. Her nose and cheeks are buried deep—under a knitted scarf, a ski mask covers her face. I've ordered the mask for her from REI; the slightest chill now turns her face bright-red. Her hands have started peeling, skin like translucent bark trailing from stems of river birch.

I've combed through reams of papers that the cancer study's doctors dumped into her lap—a grimoire of "maybes" to expect, report, survive. They mixed three drugs, each with its own way of killing quick-dividing cells, in hopes of leaving no surviving metastatic clumps. Nobody knows how these three poisons interact. Any of them could kill skin cells, cause them to flake away in the course of icy weeks.

Muffled by too much scarf, Judy waves me on ahead, her gesture clumped by fur mittens over gloves. I tug down my hood across my forehead, turn into the wind. Across the field, the shelter of beech and oak seems far and vague; bare branches blur behind a wall of whirling snow.

■ ■ ■

The dogs are staring at a log: Chipmunks have woken from their torpid trance. Spring has pushed green rosettes through last year's fallen leaves.

"I always thought I would live longer than Ivy," Judy says.

Ivy has just turned five. Judy bends down, grasps a stem, yanks, sends soil flying.

"Maybe this one is really just a cyst," I say. "They're hollow; the radiologists can see that on the scans."

Judy nods. Her gynecologist already told her this. She jerks up another tuft of greenery, a waft of garlic floats my way— here's a woman who knows exactly what she's after. I scan ahead: Leafy rosettes outline our path, renegade clumps of green scrambling into still-leafless brush.

"Just a cyst," and yet the gynecologist wants to cut and look around. I bend and pull. More garlic scent. Yips by the log, a pounce, a brief, wild chase. The chipmunk scrambles up a beech, spits defiance at the dogs below.

■ ■ ■

A windowless examination room admits no autumn sunshine, negates the dance of glowing leaves outside. There's three of us and three of them—too little space to sit and none to breathe. The surgeon's cell phone rings; he apologizes, motions his two interns to trail him out the door. White paper, from a butcher's roll, crinkles on grey vinyl as Judy shifts on the tabletop. I look at Laura. She slowly shakes her head. My head nods an agreement to her shake. They asked me along as "extra ears;" I try to refrain from being "extra mouth." But on my own, at home, I could not stop myself from being "extra eyes," could not rein in my fingers' crazy chase down keyboard paths, hot on the trails of numbers, Latin words.

Twenty percent. One in five patients receiving "thermal intraperitoneal chemotherapy," the fourteen syllables we've driven two hours to discuss, dies on the operating table. For the other four, life tends to go on two or three months longer than it would without. But—all these numbers come from patients close to death, where rampant tumors choke the body cavity. No one knows what happens if the cell clumps aren't so big, the patient not so sick and weak. No one knows the risk of pouring hot poison into the belly of a woman who yanks a hundred mustard plants on two daily walks. That's what "experimental" means, after all.

Months ago, the cyst that prompted yet another surgery was never found. But, in mid-procedure, the gynecologist called an oncologist to help: They cut a mass away from Judy's bladder wall, excised some smaller lumps, biopsied anything suspicious. After six more months of chemotherapy her scans are clear. But they have always been. Judy's tumors have a way of hiding in the brush.

This surgeon, too, has waved his hand at blurry scans: "Nothing to see," he said, as though the winding trail of Judy's colon were just a quiet woodland path. Nothing to see, and yet he wants to slice and search, pre-heated toxic cocktails within reach. Nothing to see, and yet we're here, two hours away from woods and home, not breathing as we await re-entry of this doctor and his train. The Alien Plants Working Group keeps sounding in my ear: "Because the seeds of garlic mustard can remain viable in the soil for five years or more, effective management requires a long term commitment."

"Laparoscopic doesn't mean easy," Laura says.

The surgeon, having stepped back in, agrees: "But it's the only way to have a look."

I am not breathing.

Laura's face is white, Judy's bright-red.

The vinyl of the table still is grey.

"I'll do it. For Ivy," Judy says.

■ ■ ■

Spring three: green leaves along my path sprawl heart-shaped, long-stalked, tooth-edged—and already limp. On days when work runs longer than it should I always know when Judy's walked ahead of me. Pulled and tossed on the trail's tight-tamped dirt and rock, these plants will die, unable to re-sink their drying roots. My dog is staring at that same old log: One day this chipmunk's scramble for the beech will be too slow. But not today. I tug a few rosettes, escapist renegades, a foot or two into the brush—a small addition to Judy's trail of executees.

"You know you can't get them all."

I felt I had to tell her this, one day.

"Did I ever show you my favorite cartoon?" she asked in return, her glasses twinkling, mustards dangling from her fist. I shook my head, so she explained: "There's this little girl walking down a beach, tossing starfish back into the water. And then a man tells her that she can't save them all. And she just picks up the next one, tosses it in, and says: 'Betcha I saved this one.'"

I bend again. I pull. I toss. Lightning-speed rustle through twigs and weeds; my dog leaps at the beech's smooth trunk. Furious chatter pelts from above.

■ ■ ■

"Do you think there are less of them?"

Judy scans white bouquets along the path. It's spring again. Ivy sniffs, then squats to pee.

"Yes," I say. "It sure seems that way."

The Alien Plants Working Group has never left my head: "Regardless of the control method employed, annual monitoring is necessary for a period of at least five years to ensure that seed stores of garlic mustard have been exhausted." Three years ago, the cap stayed on the heated poison pouch; the surgeon's laparoscope found nothing.

"Minimally invasive" doesn't mean "easy"—fifteen incisions slowly healed, scarring a belly like a battlefield. But Judy's scans are clear.

We stop to wait for Ivy at the wavy edge of woodland shade. Judy steps off the trail. I watch her bend, and yank, and toss. ■

QUESTIONS OF LINEAGE

How did stone ghosts
crawl along arms
and between fingers,
as men crumbled the edge
of the mountain to set steel?
Did the stone ghosts
travel in dust with every
pickax swing,
with every concussion
of dynamite? Did they travel
back home on skin to wives,
months later in the dark of winter
with children born in pain?
When did the children learn
veins carry grit, gravel grinding
between molars? How many years
until the dust was sifted
from behind eyes? And when
did sleep return from the half-
remembered color of rock?

NOAH DAVIS

CROW SONG

Wet pavement rides the ridges
up to where the forest breaks

like hair when the taut newness
of a scar writes that desire

is black feathers caught
in the heads of dried goldenrod,

that grief's blue lines run over hands
and between knuckles, that death,

after rain, leaks its sweet smell
through the river of your teeth.

NOAH DAVIS

RACCOON ON TOUCH

Bodies are easy to find in cold water.
Flesh ringed, set in the way current
cups rocks, leaving room beneath
so crayfish and minnows remain
despite the pulsing. The same beat

that sends water to the roots of catalpa,
to limbs, to leaf, to pod, to river, to crushed
shells kissing crushed shells, and paws
pausing in what swirls they can find.

NOAH DAVIS

JESSICA CHICCEHITTO HINDMAN

A mericans are less able than ever to tell the difference between real and fake," memoirist Jessica Chiccehitto Hindman says. "And we are all suffering for it."

This blunt observation about our current national moment strikes at the heart of her debut memoir, *Sounds Like Titanic*, which tells the story of her experience touring the United States as a violinist in an ensemble of musicians led by a man she calls The Composer. But there is a catch.

Unbeknownst to their audiences, the microphone is dead, and they are miming to a recording. As the strange, bewitching tale unfolds, Hindman grapples with what it means to be a woman, an Appalachian, an American, a writer, and a performer.

After a recent reading at Berea College, *Appalachian Heritage*'s Emily Masters caught up with Hindman to chat about translating music to the page, the blurred lines between reality and falsity, her views on the education system in Appalachia, and the prevailing notions of beauty and female bodies.

■ ■ ■

EMILY MASTERS: This is a fascinating memoir. You toured the country as a violinist in an ensemble that played along onstage with a dead microphone to a recording— and audiences across the country were completely fooled. When did you know you would have to write about this experience?

JESSICA CHICCEHITTO HINDMAN: Thank you! By the time I went on the fifty-three city tour around America with The Composer in 2004, I knew that this would be an experience I would write about in some way. The experience was just so absurd that I knew it would make great writing material.

EM: You grew up in the Potomac Highlands of West Virginia, which figures into the book at various points. In *Sounds Like Titanic*, you bring to light the lack of access to opportunity due to the topographical features of Appalachia. The picture you paint of education and

opportunity in the region is pretty dismal. Do you think much has changed since you were growing up and going to school in the region?

JCH: Yes, it has changed, sadly for the worse. I grew up in two very small towns in the Appalachian region—one in West Virginia, the other just over the state line in Virginia. My family moved to the town in Virginia in 1990, when the West Virginia teachers went on strike and school was cancelled for some time. The differences between those towns were immense in 1990 and are even more immense now. In recent years, my town in West Virginia was hit very hard by the opioid crisis. Despite having around 2,000 people, the town has been featured in a lot of national news stories about heroin and painkiller addiction. The last time I visited, I noticed that even some of the most basic businesses, like the 7-Eleven gas station, were boarded up and abandoned. Meanwhile, my town in Virginia has been thriving, with lots of new businesses, beautification efforts, and expanded public services such as new parks and other community activities. My Virginia town has also been featured in national news stories about the opioid crisis, but it hasn't been annihilated by that problem the way that my West Virginia town has. It is both heartbreaking and fascinating to see how two towns separated by a single mountain range have had such a different trajectory.

EM: You talk a lot about your experiences of inferiority when you left the mountains of West Virginia and Virginia due to your dialect and accent and how you felt like you had to be a spokesperson for the region as a whole while you were in college. How have you grappled with maintaining your identity as someone from the mountains

Jessica Chiccehitto Hindman
Photo: Vanessa Borer

while trying to make outsiders understand the complexity of the region? Do you still feel the pressure to speak for the people from back home?

JCH: When I first arrived in New York City, I felt a lot of pressure to explain to folks where I was from and what it was like. There were more people in my dormitory than there were in either of the towns I grew up in. I was really intimidated and felt very out of place. I quickly realized that I was a token-admission to the Ivy League, that my "job" there was to play the role of the poor kid from Appalachia. In a lot of ways, the role of the token-Appalachian kid is to make wealthy, privileged students feel better about the elitism of the school, because look—the school allows in a few kids from rural places. I really resented that role, especially because I felt I was the wrong person for it; my family was one of the most privileged in both of the towns where I grew up.

When I first got to New York, I was told I had an accent, and the reaction to that accent wasn't always positive. I got the sense that people felt like the accent represented negative things—ignorance and racism in particular—and because of that, I gradually began to speak differently. This wasn't a conscious choice, but more of a survival mechanism and sort of a way of being polite to people in New York.

I think it is very important for folks in similar situations to be aware of the role that one is expected to play in those environments and to fight against it. Unlike [*Hillbilly Elegy* author] J.D. Vance's description of Yale Law School, in which he was super impressed by the boarding-school-educated, chardonnay-swilling, northeastern elite, I found myself enraged by the vast chasm in educational opportunities and the way in which my presence there was being used as "proof" that anyone could get to the Ivy League with enough hard work. That is just false; there were many people I grew up with who were much smarter than I was who never had a chance to go to college, let alone an Ivy League school. I made it mostly because my parents were both highly educated and middle class. Appalachia isn't geographically far away from the boarding-school-areas of New England, and yet it might as well be another country.

EM: More and more people are facing issues related to massive wealth disparity caused by corporate wealth and corruption. In the final section of your memoir, you examine some of these issues including access to health care, cost of living, and making living wages. We can see that many people in Appalachia have been experiencing these economic effects since extractive industries entered the region after the Civil War. Should we as a nation have recognized what was happening in Appalachia as a warning, and should we have seen the spread of economic disparity coming?

JCH: Yes, that is an excellent way to put it. And it goes beyond Appalachia. Extractive industries have been exploiting poor and/or geographically isolated people for a long time. I'm a writer, so I think about this particularly when it comes to the publishing industry. If you want to write a book about West Virginia, and have it marketed and sold to West Virginians, you have to go through a literary agency and publishing house that is based in Manhattan. Those industries are run by coastal elites—many of whom are lovely people—but they are not representative of the country as a whole. There are lots of great small, regional presses, but none have the marketing and distribution capacities of the big New York City publishers. I think about this all the time in terms of what it does to people's stories, which stories end up getting published, and which stories get mainstream publicity and attention.

EM: In the book you write, "Life in the body means that no physical part of you—not even the lips that you have no choice but to bring with you into prealgebra class—is left unseen, unremarked upon, uncalculated for sexual potential." Your examination life in the body reveals how crippling societal pressure of what a woman should be like has been in your life. How would you advise young women going through similar recognition of life in the body to overcome those pressures and pursue their dreams?

JCH: I get the phrase "life in the body" from Naomi Wolf's book *The Beauty Myth*, which was published in the early 1990s, around the same time I began to experience what American culture is like for those who live in a female body. Wolf argued that girls my age—pre-teens at the time—were already showing "mutations" in our self-esteem, and these were due to a cultural backlash against the women's liberation movement. In other words, in exchange for greater political, civic, and professional power, the culture was going to make girls hate their own bodies. That rings very true to me. I should add that my experience is one that is inextricably linked to white privilege. Women of color have always had extra scrutiny from society on their bodies. The best thing I've read on this subject recently is Tressie McMillan Cottom's essay collection, *Thick*. It's one of the best books I've read in a long time—everyone should read it.

For about a decade now, I think that the response to the "mutations" Wolf wrote about has been to try to improve women's body image. How many times have we all heard that we should "love our bodies"? But I think that response is a

Band-Aid on a gaping wound. What I tell younger women when they ask me about this now is to do a brief cataloging of how much time, money, and energy they are spending on activities that relate to outward, physical "beauty." How many hours on the treadmill and nights spent agonizing over failed diets and time and/or money spent on skin, hair, nails, etc. And then imagine what they might be able to do if at least some of that time, energy, and money was spent on

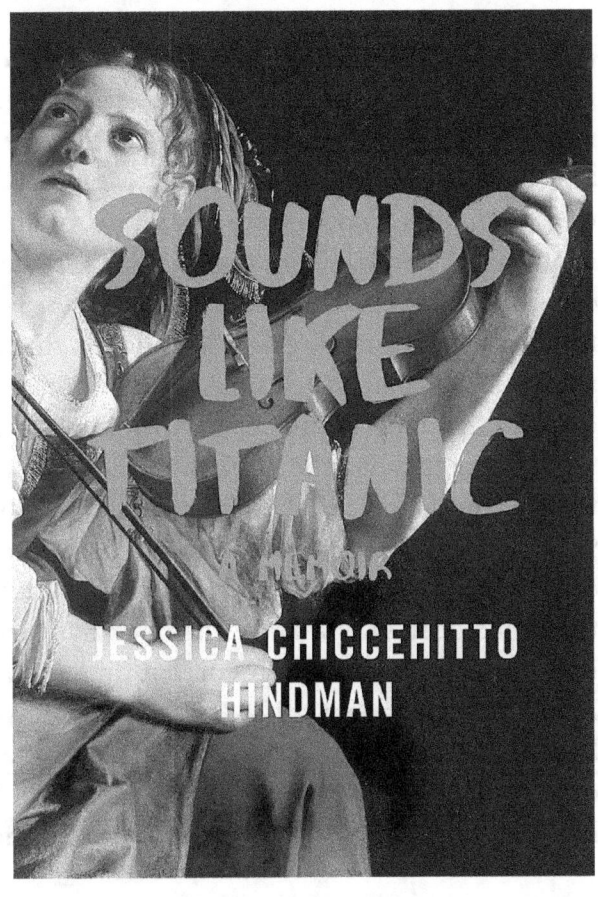

other pursuits. I try to do this myself when I go down a spiral of body-hate. What problems could I solve, what people could I help, what art could I make, if I wasn't worrying so much about being ugly and fat? It helps me turn the problem outward—into a political and cultural problem—rather than what my disordered brain and our disordered society wants me to think it is—my own personal failing of being physically unattractive.

EM: How do the economic and social issues you address in your memoir relate to events and issues going on in our current national moment?

JCH: I have been joking with people that *Sounds Like Titanic* is really my Iraq War book in disguise of a lighthearted memoir. My contention is that our nation never really had a reckoning about the trauma of 9/11. Instead, we were told to go shopping. People were desperate for anything that was soothing. When you're in that state, it's harder to tell the difference between what is real and what is fake. That leads to funny, absurd things—going to concerts that are produced by a CD—but also horrific things—supporting an invasion of a country that had nothing to do with the attacks.

When I finished the book in 2013, I thought it was going to be a "period piece," about the years immediately following 9/11. But then, in the lead-up to the 2016 election, when everyone started shouting "fake news," at each other, I realized that I had been very wrong. The book has turned out to be much more relevant to our current time than I ever imagined. I am not happy about this—I would much rather have my book be less relevant and my country be more sane. But as it turns out, Americans are less able than ever to tell the difference between real and fake. And we are all suffering for it.

EM: In the memoir, you claim, "The first lesson in making music, it turns out, is making silence—the blank canvas, the empty room, the white page. A void that must be made before it can be filled." I am interested in how that notion might translate to writing. Do you think there is a relationship between silence and writing? Where do you find your best generative space?

JCH: I'm not sure if there is a relationship between silence and writing. I like to write with minimal distractions, but I know other writers who are perfectly content to work in a noisy coffee shop or who manage to be prolific despite chaotic writing environments full of kids or pets. But I do think it's really important to acknowledge the blank page as blank. How scary it is, and yet, how freeing. Just as a musician does not need to fill every second of time with sound, a writer does not need to fill every page. It's more of figuring out what shape the words and the blank space will form. The blank spaces are just as important as the words.

EM: What were some of the challenges you faced during your writing process in bringing music to the page?

JCH: Music is a particularly challenging subject matter because music is another language. It's the equivalent of trying to write about Spanish, Arabic, or Chinese but doing so only using English words. How do you begin to describe Spanish if you can only write in English? So, when writing about music I try to use the other four senses as much as possible. I describe The Composer's music as the equivalent of a surfboard in a bathtub—too big for its structure, too obvious, too absurd. The sound of a cello can be buttery. The sound of a high-pitched flute can make a listener feel as though they are flying. The feeling of a string under your fingers is like having tiny flames shoot into your fingertips; when this happens each note in the ear is like listening to a little fire. The point is to try to stretch the language as much as possible to describe something that isn't possible to translate into straightforward description.

EM: How did you come to write creative nonfiction?

JCH: When I was in college I wanted to become a journalist. As I describe in the book, I majored in Middle Eastern Studies, began to learn Arabic, and planned to work as a foreign correspondent. The U.S. was in the process of losing two wars in the Middle East, so this seemed like a reasonable aspiration to have at the time. But the years I was in college happened to coincide with the collapse of journalism. Entire newspapers folded, and even the biggest outlets shut down most if not all of their foreign bureaus. At the same time, I was touring with The Composer, hoping to save enough money to fund my own freelance trip to the Middle East. But while I was on the tour I developed a panic disorder and realized I was no longer mentally stable enough to become a war correspondent. What I needed, instead, was to get a stable job that offered health insurance so I could get psychiatric care. I got a job as a secretary for a research institute at Columbia's medical school. The job was boring, but it offered me free tuition remission for grad school. By then, I had been reading a lot of long-form, literary reporting on the Middle East and thought that creative nonfiction might be better suited to my skills than straightforward journalism. So, I decided to apply to the School of the Arts to study creative nonfiction writing. It was there that I began to write what later became *Sounds Like Titanic.*

EM: Do you have any other writing projects in the works?

JCH: I do, but I am one of those writers who can't really speak about a project until I have a full rough draft of it down for fear of ruining it in some way. I'm in the first draft stage now and will be for a while. It's a nonfiction project, but that's about all I can say at this point. ■

I CAN'T REALLY REMEMBER

when my grandfather had me press my ear
to the steel of a bar of railroad track
to show me how you can tell
when a train's moving on the tracks
somewhere down the line. I can't
bring up how the steel was ground shiny
smooth in spots, then grimy with rust
and coal power at the same time
against my tiny and curious ear.
How I shook the dust from my hair
when I stood up. Can't fully track the vision
of how I thought I felt the vibration
with my fingers, too. Wasn't sure
if it was something I'd heard,
or was only feeling. I can't tell
if what I feel now is that same feeling
of being given over a kind of secret
by him. Like an accidental trick
he'd only figured out when he was eight
and had been waiting a long time
to tell someone about.

LARRY D. THACKER

WAITING FOR DEER

I feel a tingling that begins in the wrists
and spreads with the joy of them.
                        —Richard Taylor

When they come, circumspect as they need to be,
the metal feeder is there for them,
two payoff slots of easy bounty.

I am the quiet watcher, my only motion moving
these words across the page.

Two does, their hide this time of year
the color of deep smoke.
They bend to the rice bran, corn, protein mix,
then look my direction. Something not quite right
in the shadows, but perhaps harmless.

I wish they knew how beautiful they are
in their sleek coats, dexterous tongues
now swiping up the pellets.

I knew a man once who hoped for this closeness
so he could drag a deer home. Not here.
But they are suddenly spooked by our neighbor's
chainsaw grinding the air . . .

The deer pause, eye each other, then bend again
to the ground where, always in the moment,
they find a little more to go on.

JEFF WORLEY

THE HUNT

CATHY CRUISE

When he asks "Shotgun?" it takes her a second to realize he's not wondering where she wants to sit in the truck, but what weapon she wants to bring.

Lizzie wrinkles her nose. He knows she doesn't like guns. "Bow," she says, and yanks on the door. She has to yank hard and still it opens slowly, moaning like a wounded animal.

She slides across the cold seat and watches in the rearview mirror as her father places the crossbow in the back of the pickup, moving aside the rolled sleeping bags he always brings. It's dark already—the time fell back last weekend—but they left the trailer lights on to spill across the driveway. It's enough so Lizzie can see her father's thin face, dark beard, his John Deere hat. He slams the hatch shut and gets in beside her.

"Head over to Darnell?" He starts the engine. "Check that valley again?"

He backs out of the gravel drive and then they're on the road that leads to the highway. No doubt it leads other places too, but Lizzie doesn't know where just yet.

There hasn't been much neighborhood exploring since they moved here two months ago, at the end of summer, the end of everything. When her mother died in August, her father declared they were getting out of Ohio quick, and Lizzie didn't argue. But why West Virginia? That's what she'd asked then, and still does, even though she knows the answer. A job. For parents, it's always a job. But so far, this job seems to be just ahead of them. Her father's forever waiting on a call, going for an interview, turning in paperwork. Meantime he cuts trees and mows grass, delivers hay to farms nearby. When Lizzie asks about the job, he says, "You just be you. I'll just be me."

So she is just her, even when it's hard to be. And he's just him. And sometimes, like tonight, they're just them, off on the hunt.

As they speed along I-64, a breeze picks up and a white moon appears above the mountains, among the stars. There are so many stars here.

"Make a wish, Liz," her mom used to say, in the evenings, when the first light appeared in the blue-black sky. Her hand had cupped Lizzie's knee as they sat on their brick patio at the duplex in Canton. They shared the patio with the Issings, Bud and Rachel, and their two boys. The Issings hardly ever used their side of the space, but Lizzie and her mom would sit there in the early evenings, in two old lawn chairs Lizzie's dad had found along the road. He'd replaced the webbing, and they were as pretty and comfortable as new on summer nights, perfect for sitting beneath the stars, wishing.

Lizzie wonders now what happened to those chairs. She would like to have one of them. Not both, though. Because she would never want to sit and look at the empty one.

"How was math today?" her father asks. "Was your test hard?"

She thinks about the problems she worked today that were from third grade, a whole year ago. "No. They're behind here."

"What about the Jesus class?"

Lizzie picks at a jagged nail. It keeps catching on things, so she bites at it.

"What happened? They let you out, right?"

Lizzie nods. "I had art instead. We made foil sculptures."

She was startled by how easy the lie slid out like that.

After lunch yesterday, Lizzie's fourth day of school here, her teacher Miss Burke had announced it was time for Bible studies. She handed Lizzie a book called *Growing with God*, and told the class to turn to page sixty-four.

Lizzie opened the book. A cartoon of a man took up nearly the whole page. He wore leaves around his waist and was plunging down the back of a dinosaur. The caption beneath it read: "Imagine how Adam might have crawled up on the back of a Brontosaurus. He and Eve could have their own personal water slide! Wouldn't that be so wild!"

Lizzie had let out a laugh, then felt her face go warm when everyone looked at her.

"It's a funny picture, isn't it, Lizzie?" Miss Burke asked. She was short, with red glasses that just matched her hair.

"No," Lizzie said. "Well, yes. But…dinosaurs lived millions of years before people."

A boy beside her threw his hand in the air.

"Yes, Dwayne?" Miss Burke asked.

He pointed at Lizzie. "She believes in evolution."

The class erupted in whispers until Miss Burke told everyone to settle down.

"Lizzie since you're new here, I'll explain about this class. Every Thursday afternoon, we study God's word. The Bible. And the Bible teaches us that men and women were created at the very beginning, when the Earth was brand new."

Lizzie blinked. "But what about science? What about dinosaur bones, and fossils?"

Becky Kinder turned around to face her. She sat in front of Lizzie, and had creamy pink cheeks, and deep green eyes beneath dark bangs. Lizzie had hoped she and Becky would become best friends.

"Those things are put here to test our faith," Becky said. "Ain't that right, Miss Burke?"

"Okay." Miss Burke said. "Let's get back to our lesson."

After school Lizzie had told her dad about the Bible class. She'd thought it was funny, and hoped he'd laugh. She tried everything to make him laugh these days. But he'd only slammed cabinets in the kitchen while he made dinner, and this morning he'd walked into school with Lizzie to talk to the principal, a bald man in a dark suit, about how his daughter wasn't going to be taught a bunch of nonsense.

The man beamed and spread his arms wide. "It's an elective!" he said. "She doesn't have to attend."

Lizzie was sent not to art class, but to the library.

Miss Burke directed her to a table behind the reference stacks. "You can read your book if you'd like." She'd nudged her glasses up higher on her nose and halfway smiled at Lizzie, like maybe she was feeling guilty, sticking her in there all alone. But she left anyway, and then the room was empty except for Mrs. Daniels, the librarian, who sat at the front desk and never talked and didn't like anyone else to either.

It was cold in the library, and smelled moldy and damp. Lizzie opened her own book, *Harry Potter and the Prisoner of Azkaban*, thinking how her father would have a fit if he knew she were just sitting here reading instead of learning something new. She decided not to tell him, and prayed he wouldn't find out. Then she started giggling. Kicked out of Bible class and here she was, praying.

Now her father flips on his turn signal, and they head off the highway onto a gravel road that soon turns to dirt. The shocks groan when they brake at a flat spot in the grass. He shuts off the engine.

Lizzie climbs out and lifts her backpack from the truck bed. She keeps it packed full—two flashlights, two bottled

Lizzie follows him into the nearest section of woods. The afternoon rain has made the ground soft, and the air smells like mud.

waters, a camera, lap blanket, knife, rope, compass, and a lighter. Tonight she's added a sandwich—peanut butter and sardines.

Her dad lifts out the crossbow, and Lizzie follows him into the nearest section of woods. The afternoon rain has made the ground soft, and the air smells like mud.

Darnell was the first place they'd picked when they moved here, chosen for the high hills and low valleys they could see from the highway, and the scattered patches of dense woods between. But now, in the beam of her flashlight, Lizzie can only see worn grass and the knotted roots of trees beneath her sneakers.

"Watch your step," her father says. His voice isn't quite a whisper, but it's hoarse, always softer than usual out here. He's slung the bow across his back and he holds onto its wide strap with one hand.

They come out from the trees into a deep valley. Lizzie can hear the little stream in front of them, and she heads toward their first trap, strung over the wet rocks between two scraggly white pines.

Her father stoops down so she can climb onto his shoulders, and suddenly she's up high, swaying for a startling second, before he regains his balance. But his grip on her calves is steel. She knows he would never let her fall.

She shines the light into the dark sky, looking for the rope they'd hung weeks ago. "Move right," she says. "Wait. There it is."

Above her head, within reach if she stretches, is the mesh laundry bag holding a sandwich, or what's left of it. Her father moves sideways so Lizzie can grab hold. She untangles the damp bread from the bag and inspects it before she hands it down to him.

"Well, something got it," he says. "Those teeth marks? There in the corner?"

"Probably birds," she says.

She's glad she can't see his face when she says this, because she wouldn't want to see the disappointment there. Lizzie wants more than anything to find something, but not so much for her. If they're ever successful, she thinks, it might just put the light back in her dad's eyes.

He flings the sandwich into the stream.

Lizzie slides her backpack off her shoulder, just enough so she can pull out the new sandwich—this time made with a thick, chewy sourdough, baked by their neighbor Mrs. Eades, who brings them a fresh loaf every couple of weeks. Lizzie places it in the bag just right, so it stays flat but still swings around in the breeze. The bag is black, almost invisible against the dark sky, so the sandwich looks like it's floating there, like in a Scooby-Doo cartoon.

"Done?" her father asks.

She is, but she isn't ready to come down just yet. It's her favorite part of the hunt, being up high like this, smelling the clear night air, feeling it on her face. Now she can see past the stream, across the rocky bottom of the valley, encircled by the black slopes of mountains that look like sleeping giants. When she's like this, connected to her dad, but seeing the open world from up high, it's almost like she's a whole new creature—tall, strong, fierce.

But she can feel her father's weight shift, like he's getting tired, so she tells him she's done and he sets her down.

He walks to an incline at their left. "Let's try this way."

Lizzie follows him, reminding herself to make an entry of this when she gets back to the truck. She keeps a notebook beneath the seat, which has all their information from every hunt, so they never repeat themselves, and never forget.

It was the promise of these Friday night hunts that made Lizzie excited about this move. Her father had told her stories of sightings in West Virginia, in woods so thick a creature could stay hidden from humans for decades, and grow, even breed. He'd thrilled her with talk of running, hiking, hiding, capturing. All things they could never do in Canton. And it had been fun so far, even if they hadn't found a thing.

Not that she expected to. She wasn't a little kid anymore. But, just like the library, she would never tell her dad that. He believed in the hunt. She believed in him.

As they head up the hill, her father picks up a long, fat stick. He says it's a walking stick, but she knows it's more for protection, in case he can't grab the bow in time.

She doesn't worry about that. The woods feel safe to her. It's out in the rest of the world that things get risky. Just look at her mom, who died in that car wreck. Who went out one night with her friend, Tammy, and never came home.

Her father stops and points with the stick to the right side of the trail.

"What is it?" she asks. But she can already see the indentation, probably a foot long, half a foot wide, sunk an inch into the mud. "Any more?"

She shines the light ahead, and her father gazes up the hill for a long moment. Lizzie studies the nearby bushes for tangles of hair, broken branches, spots that make good sleeping nests. She sniffs for scat, but smells only the cold night air, hinting at what could be a first snow.

"Might be a print," he says.

"Not big enough." She's told him this before. Most are at least two feet long.

"Could be a young'un," he says, moving up the hill.

She wants to point out that there would be more tracks, but she lets it drop.

They wind upward, around the rocky parts, all the while avoiding the ledge at their right, which her father keeps a constant watch on. It's funny, she thinks, how he always walks along the edge himself, and forces her to the inside. Even now he presses his hand to her shoulder and nudges her over.

He walks without talking, leaning on his stick. Moonlight outlines his head and his thin, slumped shoulders. When a cloud shifts and the sky brightens for just an instant, she can see his expression, the features dark and sad.

She loves him so much it hurts. A real, physical pain in her chest that spreads to her throat and stings her eyes.

She hears his foot slide, the crunching sound of rocks and dirt skidding beneath his shoe. Even before he yelps and grabs out, Lizzie dives for him and grasps his arm. The next thing she knows she's falling, face forward, into a black nothing.

The night sky spins for an instant, the few stars in motion now, leaving trails, like in that painting, *Starry Night*. And then they're tumbling down the hillside, helplessly crashing against the ground and into one another.

It only lasts a few seconds, thankfully, before they crash into a thicket of Mountain Laurel and come to a stop.

It's so quiet. After the rolling and tumbling Lizzie is amazed to hear only the soft rush of wind above them. They lie still, breathing hard, staring at the stars, now still again, pulsing.

"Liz," her father groans. "Lizzie!" He crawls to her and touches her cheek, the top of her head. "You okay?"

He picks up her hands and peers at her palms, lifts each of her legs and bends them at the knee. After a minute, he barks out a laugh. "Not a scratch on you!" And then he laughs some more, sitting beside her, hanging his head between his knees.

She hasn't heard him laugh in months. She should be glad, she guesses, but it's a strange sound, and scary, because his shoulders are shaking like he can't help himself, and all of a sudden she wonders if he's still laughing after all.

Lizzie lies still on the cold ground. She nearly just lost her father. Up here in the dark, alone, and what would she have done then?

Harry Potter is an orphan. In her book, he's running from Sirius Black, although he shouldn't be, as it turns out. Sirius is a good guy, practically a relative, but Harry doesn't know this yet. Lizzie does, because this is her third time reading it. Today, when they were packing up at dismissal, Becky Kinder saw the book and told Lizzie, "You don't need to be reading that. You need to read the Bible."

Lizzie had studied Becky for a minute, decided they'd never be friends anyway, so she folded her arms across her chest. "New or Old Testament?" she'd asked.

Becky stared at her.

"Which books? What verses are your favorites?"

Red splotches bloomed onto Becky's round cheeks and her eyes traveled over Lizzie, down to her shoes, then up to her face again. "Freak," she hissed, before she walked away.

Lizzie had felt good at the time. Ever since, she's felt anything but. Now she's lying here, listening to her father's crazy laughter, staring at the starry sky and feeling sad that Becky Kinder hates her, and that she cares that Becky hates her. Mostly, though, she's sad Becky and her friends don't know about Harry Potter, or maybe anything that doesn't involve God, or Adam, or dinosaurs.

Her father runs his fingers across his face. Then he coughs and pushes himself up. He reaches for her hand.

They climb the steep hillside, holding onto bare shrubs and rocks as they go. At the top, her father hoists himself onto the landing, then reaches for Lizzie and pulls her up behind him, as easily as Hagrid would. Then they stand at the cliff's edge, breathing, for what seems like a long time. Her father turns to look at her. "I'm sorry, hon."

She puts her arms around his waist and pulls him toward her. Her heart is pounding and the dank cold is making her nose run. But if she sniffs, he'll think she's crying. She feels like crying, she realizes.

"I'm freezing," she says.

"I know. But we can still head to the top. We're almost there." He untangles her hands and steps back from her.

"I want to go home."

"Let's at least get to the ...."

"I don't want to do this anymore," she says.

Her dad struggles to smile, but it ends up like always, in a sad, sideways frown. "What do you mean?"

"I want to go home," she says. "This is stupid."

He scratches his face, rubs his hand along his beard. "Well now. Come on. You have to believe."

Why, she wants to ask. Why does she have to believe? In the hunt? In magic, evolution, heaven? Anything? For the first time, she knows for certain this is all for nothing. She looks up at his face, and that pain swells in her chest again, that sweet ache of love, so big she can hardly bear it. She can't tell her father she knows. She can't do anything except swallow and breathe and try not to cry.

And then she hears the sound. It's a deep, trilling moan, from just over the top of the ridge. It makes the hair on the back of her neck stand up. She's never heard anything like it.

Her father slowly looks down at her, wide-eyed, and then before she can even think, she breaks out in a run. He makes a grab for her, but she swerves away and tears up the hillside,

Why, she wants to ask. Why does she have to believe? In the hunt? In magic, evolution, heaven? Anything?

toward the sound, her heart beating fast and her chest aching from the cold air rushing in and out.

"Lizzie!" Her father's voice is hoarse and panicked. But she keeps going, up and up. She won't stop until she's at the very top, and even then she imagines going on, over the other side and down it, full tilt. She can already feel how fast the hill would speed her toward it, to whatever it is. And she's ready. She wants to meet it head-on.

But when she clears the top of the ridge, she slams to a stop. There is no hillside, only a sharp drop-off, inches away from her toes. Lizzie stares at the open space in front of her, her breath huffing in and out, making clouds that mist up and vanish.

Her father reaches her a second later, grabs her by the shoulders and pulls her away from the edge. "Don't," he huffs. "Don't do that. Scared me."

She twists away from him and shines her flashlight down the cliff. The weak yellow beam lights up bushes and rocks, trees and grass, but only so far. What's outside that light, in the vast dark, is huge and mysterious, and far out of her reach.

"Let's go," her father says. "It's time to go."

Lizzie swallows hard. "But it's out there," she says.

Her father stands still beside her, the only sound now the creak of branches in the wind. "I know. But it's moved on."

He takes Lizzie's hand, turns her toward him, and peers at her face. "Let's get home, Liz," he says. His eyes are clear and searching, tilted in their sad arch.

Lizzie stares out at the drop-off, at the black space all around her. Then she lets her father pull her by the hand, and they start back down the hill.

And it ends the way it always does, with the two of them back in the pickup truck, waiting for the stalled heater to warm them, jostling along the dark highway as Lizzie writes by flashlight in her notebook, her pen making soft scratching noises. But tonight, she can't concentrate, and stops mid-sentence to gaze out her window, watching the moon rise and the clouds roll back in, as murky and cautious as ghosts.

■ ■ ■

The next Thursday, Mrs. Daniels is out sick, so the library is closed. Miss Burke apparently doesn't want to risk a Bible study with Lizzie there, so she rolls a television into the room, high on a metal stand, and turns on a show called *Veggie Tales*. It's about talking vegetables. In this one a tomato and a cucumber defeat a lying garden weed. The vegetables talk about truth, and what it says in the Bible about real versus make believe.

It's kind of a babyish show, Lizzie thinks, but the other kids seem to enjoy it. When it's over, Miss Burke asks them questions—what they thought was funny and what they learned. As she's unplugging the television and wrapping up the cord, she bends down to Lizzie and says, "You're awfully quiet lately."

Lizzie nods, because she doesn't know how else to respond.

"Can I ask you something, honey?" Miss Burke leans in close. Lizzie can smell her flowery cologne. "Do you believe in God?"

She meant to ask privately, Lizzie knows, but she can feel every child in the room stiffen to attention. It's so quiet, she can hear the deep mumble of Mr. Reef, lecturing his class next door.

Becky Kinder twists around in her chair and stares at her. But Lizzie looks straight at Miss Burke, at her glasses glinting under the lights.

She thinks of her mother, in the cozy lawn chair, her head tilted back to look up at the stars. And those tumbling stars the other night, when she and her father could have both died, out in the forest alone, and not a soul would have known, or maybe even cared. Would God have seen? And if so, why wouldn't He have reached out a hand to stop them?

Or did He?

She lets out a breath. "Yes," she says.

Miss Burke tilts her head, and a smile spreads across her face. "Well, okay then," she says, and turns back toward the TV.

Lizzie watches her place the cord on the stand and unlock the wheels at the bottom. Just as she starts to roll it away, Lizzie raises her hand. "Miss Burke?"

She turns to her. "Yes, hon?"

Lizzie lowers her hand. She looks Becky Kinder straight in the eyes. "I do believe in God," she says. "But then again, I believe in Bigfoot." ■

COSMOGONY

Down into the waters,
like Beowulf to Grendel's grave,
goes the beetle,
diving and rising again and again
through a churned sea
with tiny mouthfuls of mud.
He's building the slow island
where we will live,
moving unscathed through boiling waters
to deposit land, land, Heorot home,
open to the stone arch of sky.
There is balance; he does not puncture it
to make this place,
though earth floats between
that vault and the teeming sea,
suspended at north, south, east, and west
down lines like the ribs of a basket.

LAURA SCHAFFER

THE CLUBHOUSE

It was never a revolution, never a rebellion
against household expectations—
only two children supported

by chimney bricks, the intrepid stitch
of youth threading limbs together.
Three stories and we weren't afraid

of falling, afraid our feet could stumble
past gutters, afraid the neighbors
might notice two brothers alight the roof,

circle, and climb inside again. We were only scared our
parents might hear bare feet over shingles,
          so we tiptoed.

We stood against the horizon of hundred-year-old
houses, holding on to the invulnerability given
by the distance to the ground.

                              IAN C. WILLIAMS

TIME
CAPSULE

BRE LILLIE

My family's home was located at the bottom of a gently sloping hill, just outside the wooden fence that surrounded the trailer park. This was a distinction my mom was always careful to make when giving directions to our house. On the phone with friends she'd say, "Yes, it's just off Blythewood Road," and then with a sigh she would concede that it was in fact near Duval's Mobile Home Park.

I never could figure out why it bothered my mom so much to live near the park. We only lived there at all because my grandma had married into the Duval family at the age of forty. This second marriage of hers provided her with a rich contractor husband who owned a lake house and had a knack for giving extravagant gifts.

Growing up I never knew what a regular work schedule looked like, and that typical fathers had them. There were only three types of men I ever encountered in my small life near the trailer park. There were the factory workers who worked twelve-hour shifts and came home to drink beer in their recliners and fall asleep with the baseball game on. There were people like my step grandpa, Buck Duval, who I never saw lift a finger to actually do anything but was intimidating enough to make anyone follow his orders. And then there were people like my dad, who worked as the manager of sorts for Duval's, looking out for his stepfather's properties by acting as stand-in plumber, electrician, and rent collector, as needed. It was a good job for him. He couldn't do anything on a schedule, so he was better suited to aimlessly wandering the park, giving everyone he passed a vague smile before disappearing, often for hours at a stretch, to write in the small ragged notebook he carried in his left back pocket.

My understanding of women was similarly limited to my local area. There were moms like my own, who worked, cooked, and did laundry. Then there were women very unlike my mom, such as my grandma. Whenever Grandma showed up in her cherry cough syrup colored Buick with my eleven-year-old aunt Brandy in tow, I had no idea that all grandmothers didn't have big blond hair with dark brown lowlights and teal and silver inch-long fingernails.

My aunt Brandy was not a person you could say no to. She was four years my senior, and even at the age of eleven whenever she wanted something it appeared before her almost before she finished asking for it. She was pale, skinny, brown-haired, and freckled, with braces and a slew of bad ideas.

My family believed in traditions. Every Christmas went the same way, with meals marking our progress through the day: doughnuts for breakfast, holiday party leftovers for lunch, and dinner at the lake house with Grandma. Grandma always dropped her daughter off with us right after Brandy finished opening her mound of Christmas presents. My child-aunt had to be out from under her mother's feet while she explored the kitchen she only entered during the holidays. I had a suspicion that most of our holiday dinner was prepared by the local grocery store, but Grandma still needed enough time to put everything into her expensive serving dishes and sip pink Moscato while watching movie marathons on television.

■ ■ ■

We were all outside, except for Mom. She was inside vacuuming like it wasn't Christmas at all, but just some other Tuesday. It was a warm day, almost seventy degrees, and we took advantage of the respite from winter.

Grandma pulled into the driveway, laying on the horn as she made her way up the path. Mom came outside and said, "Honey, put your dogs away." My dad didn't move from his perch at the wooden picnic table that sat just outside our front door but motioned for my older brother Keen to keep the growling bulldogs away from the car.

The two matriarchs said their brief hellos, each desiring to get back to their respective domains. Mom and Grandma were not tall, and that was where the similarities ended. When Grandma stepped out of the car in her spiked heels, I always looked at the goddess smiling down at me and wondered how my mother had caught my dad's eye. If it's true that sons marry women like their mothers, my dad must have run in the opposite direction to find his wife.

On this particular Christmas Brandy came with a stack of new toys to keep her entertained while she slummed it with us. She hopped out of the car and wisped over to half hug her half-brother where he sat at the old picnic table. She waved goodbye to her mother, saying "See you later," with a wide smile. Once her mother was out of sight, Brandy turned to my dad and said, "It feels like I haven't been here in months."

"You were here on Thursday, Bran Muffin," my dad said.

"I missed you all so much," Brandy said.

"What do you want, Sis?" my dad asked.

"You got any Pop Tarts?" she asked. "I'll share with Olive and Keen."

"Well, yeah, since those are their snacks to begin with. Kids, one of you go tell your mother I said you can have some."

My brother glanced at me and caught the baseball he'd tossed in the air without looking at it. We fought a brief but fiery battle of wills before I sighed and unseated myself from the picnic table, pausing to look back for support before venturing closer to the house, and receiving none, pressing onward to grasp the screen door. We avoided being in small, enclosed spaces with Mom individually, since she was kind of unpredictable during that period.

I emerged victorious after receiving a sighed affirmation from my mother. Brandy decided she was interested in speaking to me when she saw the metallic plastic packaging in my hands. "Hey Olive, you want to see my new doll?"

I wasn't normally a girly girl, but a few weeks before Mom had told my brother and me that we weren't getting a new little sibling at the start of the summer after all, so babies were a topic of interest for me. I couldn't understand why Dad had been coming home with bouquets of sunflowers, Mom's favorite–though goodness knows where he'd found them in midwinter–but I knew there must be some correlation between the two events.

"Sure. Thanks Bran," I said.

"Be careful. Her face is porcelain," Brandy said as she wiped crumbs from her mouth.

"Tell your mom I'm taking the dogs for a walk," my dad said as he stood up from the bench and waded through the animals sitting near his feet. He whistled, and the dogs lifted their heads in unison, but stayed where they were as he stuck his hands in his pockets and ambled down our long dirt driveway.

I stroked the doll's hair and said, "She's so pretty." This doll was exquisite. She was delicate, with big green eyes. She had chestnut colored ringlets that bounced, and I found myself frustrated by how I wasn't getting a new little sister-doll to play with.

I imagined a little pill, remembering the week before when the pharmacist told Mom to take one capsule with dinner and to call if things got worse.

"Yeah, Mama said she came from Charleston. I liked the one I got last year better, until I dropped her off the pier," Brandy said.

I said, "Her eyes close when you lean her back."

She said, "The one from last year had red hair."

I said, "The flowers on her dress match her eyes."

Brandy said, "I wish I'd gotten a dirt bike instead of all these kid toys."

I said, "I wish I was still getting a little sister."

Keen turned the corner from where he'd been circling around the house tossing the ball right as I said this. He stopped short and glanced toward the screen door. "Olive, don't say that so loud. She'll hear you," he said, jerking his head toward the house.

"You all know what a time capsule is?" Brandy asked before I could reply to Keen. I imagined a little pill, remembering the week before when the pharmacist told Mom to take one capsule with dinner and to call if things got worse. Mom didn't sleep much then.

"Of course. You take stuff you like and then bury it deep for people who'll find it in like a thousand years," Keen said.

"Let's make one," said Brandy.

"What're we going to put in it? All our stuff's in the house," I said.

"We can bury some of the things I brought. You go look around for something of yours. Keen, you still want that old baseball?"

■ ■ ■

The shed stood at the corner of the property like a tired sentinel, only remaining standing by sheer force of will. Years of paint peeled off of it in in brittle curls of red, grey, whitewash, and sage green. The awning that reached out from the shed stored a rusted I-beam, spare branches from a fake Christmas tree, several half empty bottles of Turtle Wax, decaying sheets of plywood, rolls of old linoleum and chicken wire, a red plastic cup full of nails and screws, an old car battery, and a big railroad crossing sign. I knew none of my stuff was out there, so I threw all my weight into opening the door to the shed itself.

The inside had never been painted and was dark, dull, and damp. There were cans of varnish, sealed shut by their once clear liquid contents. There was a mallet left by one of the roofers who'd re-shingled the house. There was a full bag of cat litter, which made no sense to me because we'd never owned a cat. I went straight to the very back, where old shelving had made a snug home for several generations of mice. Behind the droppings and the cobwebs was the low shelf that hid my outside treasures: Cheerwine bottle caps, a piece of gravel shaped like an arrowhead, a collection of my dad's flat carpenter pencils —mostly just little stubs— a blue jay feather, a Hot Wheels 1976 Greenwood Corvette, stained red Popsicle sticks with jokes on them, rolled bits of stripped copper wiring, and leftover strands of Mom's crocheting yarn.

I came back with my selection and found Brandy's contributions in a pile. Horrified, I saw the doll had made the cut. "If I lose her they'll just buy me another one," she said.

We couldn't find a suitable container to put the stuff in, so we dumped Dad's garden supplies out of their cardboard box near the dog kennel and placed our treasures inside. When it came time to put the doll in, I said, "Don't shove her in like that. You'll smush her hair. Let's put her in last."

Brandy shrugged and we set off to find the right place for burial. Keen knelt down and tested the soil in several parts of the backyard while Brandy and I followed with solemn presence, with her carrying the box and me clutching the doll to my chest.

The three of us formed a loose triangle, staring at the patch of dirt that was to be our burial ground. I imagine we would have made an odd sight, if anyone had been around to notice. I was wearing green penguin-covered Christmas socks pulled up almost to my knees, tennis shoes, and my old softball uniform with a hand-me-down hoodie zipped over it.

Keen had on Dad's work gloves, several sizes too large for him, with which he periodically stopped to wipe his brow, leaving soil stains on his forehead. Brandy, with her red pants, black t-shirt, and red Chuck Taylors to match, looked ready for the mall, or maybe for Hell.

One pitch of the shovel blade at the rough ground told us what we should have realized. Despite the unseasonably warm weather of the day, the soil was still frozen solid about two inches down, due to the preceding month of cold weather. No amount of cussing or leaping on the shovel's head could help Keen make a dent in the red dirt. Once my brother had used his full repertoire of swear words –at the time a relatively short list–we searched out other options. We considered the compost pile, but Keen thought we might awaken some slumbering snakes. We looked at the oak tree, but no one felt much like climbing it to see if a crevice could be found. Besides, Brandy insisted that something above ground defeated the purpose of the whole endeavor. Finally, she snapped her fingers and said, "I know where to put it. Follow me."

She led us via a circuitous route–to heighten the suspense, I imagine–and finally stopped near the azalea bushes at the back of the house. The bushes were no more than brown sticks at that time of year, so we could see clearly when she pointed to the grate that lay just beyond them, at the base of the red bricks of the house. "Here," she said with triumph.

"We're not allowed under the house," I said.

"That grate might be awfully hard to pry off," Keen said. "Olive go get me the crowbar out of the shed."

"Why do I have to get it?"

"'Cause Brandy found the spot and I'm doing the muscle work. Now go."

A few minutes later I handed my brother a large flathead screwdriver and said, "This is all I could find." I'd taken a moment to hide the crowbar on my low shelf in the shed, stacking some cans of varnish and paint samples in front of it. As the youngest child in the family, my revenge often had to be small, and just as often it went completely unnoticed.

It took nearly half an hour. Dad didn't come home. When I peeked in the window Mom had turned off the vacuum and sat watching TV with her ironing board in front of her. She didn't notice the scraping sounds of metal on metal as they mixed with flying curses that escaped Keen's mouth.

With a final grunt from my brother, the grate popped free. We took a silent inventory of the box in preparation. Keen put

I peeped through the window above the grate and saw my mom staring at the television as steam emitted from the iron in steady puffs.

his faded baseball, a stick with a bunch of notches carved in it by his pocket knife, and a piece of one of the dogs' rubber toys that gave a brief but shrill squeak as he dropped it in. I put in my pencil and a ball of mismatched yarn bits. Brandy put in an unopened deck of cards, a pack of glittery gel pens, and laid the doll on top. Right before closing the lid, Brandy said, "We should get some food to put in. They might wonder what we ate back then."

"I'm not going in the house," Keen said.

"Fine. I'll go. You two keep watch," Brandy said and slipped silently toward the back door, where the kitchen jutted off from the rest of the house. Keen went and stood right outside the door, waiting to assist Brandy with her haul. Balancing on my toes, I peeped through the window above the grate and saw my mom staring at the television as steam emitted from the iron in steady puffs. I jumped a little when she turned her head toward the kitchen, but she just nodded in that direction and returned to her vigil of the screen. Brandy returned a moment later with Keen following, her arms laden with a mismatched assortment of food.

"What'd you say to Mom?" Keen asked as she began dropping items into our time capsule. There was the last pack of strawberry Pop Tarts, a baked sweet potato wrapped in aluminum foil, half of an almond-encrusted cheese ball, cranberry sauce in a Ziploc bag, an open canister of Ready Whip, a bag of Cool Ranch Doritos, a handful of green candy canes, and a few slices of the glazed ham we were bringing to Christmas dinner wrapped up in a napkin.

"I told her I wanted a snack," Brandy said.

I felt the sudden urge that we all ought to say a few words. I remembered the pencil stub I'd put in the box and ran over to the trashcan to find a scrap of paper. I explained how we needed to leave our words behind, as well as our things, and passed the pencil to Keen, who passed it to Brandy when he was done. I took a moment to scribble my own thoughts down and asked that each person read theirs out loud.

Keen cleared his throat and said, "Um, this is our stuff. We hope you like it and if you're aliens we hope you know what it is."

Brandy said, "These are the words of Brandy Grace Duval. Here lie her precious tokens, bestowed on her by those who held her in affection and for whom she was a great joy."

I said, "If you find this, I hope you're one of my family members from the future. Good luck with everything."

The moment of burial was upon us. "How are we going to put it inside?" Keen asked.

"Olive's small. She'll fit," said Brandy.

"She's afraid of bugs."

"Oh she'll be fine. Won't you, Olive?" said Brandy.

I was very much afraid, but Keen's doubt and Brandy's affirmation spurred me on. "I can do it," I said as I took off my jacket and draped it over a bush. I took a moment to pull my socks above my knees and dropped to the ground, grabbing the box and angling it so I could push it in front of me as I crawled into the depths. One moment the sun was shining brightly on my hair and shoulders and the next the only light streamed in between the few inches my body didn't take up in the opening.

Keen's muffled voice asked, "You okay, Olive?" I kicked my foot in reply and used my elbows to drag myself further in. The surface under me was black plastic sprinkled with lime, to keep moisture out of the house above me. Good, I thought, the doll will stay dry. I didn't dare admit it to myself, but an idea of me crawling back under the house to rescue the doll raced through my head right then. I kept pushing the box and dragging myself forward until my feet touched the grate opening, and at that moment I found I could go no further. I was acutely aware of my heart pounding in my ears. I heard a floorboard creaking above me and Keen's urgent whisper of, "Come out. Mom's in the kitchen and she might see us through the doorway." I imagined what it must look like out there: two kids crouching beside a low hole in the side of the house, while little more than a set of ankles and tennis shoes jutted out through it. I pushed the box to the very tips of my fingers and scuffled backwards into the sunlight as quickly as I could.

This accomplished, we were about to put the grate back in place when Mom called through the screen door that lunch was ready. Promising to shove it back in later, Keen just propped the grate over the hole and we headed inside. I was nervous when I saw Mom pulling leftovers out of the fridge, but she didn't notice the diminished supply of rations, so we tucked in with the gusto of hungry coal miners.

■ ■ ■

I didn't think much about it. Apparently, neither did Keen. We just went about our post-Christmas lives the next day. I read one of my new books cover to cover in one sitting. Keen flipped through the setup manual of his new Sega Dreamcast. Dad walked the dogs again and came back with chocolate covered pecans for us all.

Grandma called the house and told my mom that she'd "had a hard week and just needed to let loose a little," so Brandy got dropped off at our house that afternoon so she could spend the night with us while her mother went downtown for the evening. Brandy came in toting her favorite red pillow, a red-checkered backpack, a box of Bottle Caps, and a brand new Gameboy Color. She dumped her stuff in my room and came back into the living room, plopped down in the recliner I'd been reading in until I'd had to answer the door to let her in, and proceeded to ignore Keen and me.

Mom did laundry. She scrubbed the bathtub. When I walked into the kitchen for a glass of apple juice, she was standing with her purple rubber cleaning gloves submerged in sink water. She didn't hear me open the fridge. She just stared out the window without blinking. I went back to my book, choosing a new place of residence on the couch.

■ ■ ■

I'm not certain whether it was the cold or the noise that woke me up late that night. On the one hand, Brandy had stolen all the blankets but the thin sheet on my full-size bed, wrapping herself in a cocoon of comforter and fleece throw. On the other hand, it may have been the sound of my mom and dad in the hallway having a heated conversation that pulled me from my slumber.

"…breaking into the house. I keep hearing this shuffling sound but I can't tell where it's coming from," Mom said.

"There's no one breaking in. The dogs would be barking," Dad said.

"Shush. Hear that? That crunching noise?"

"I think it's coming from under the house. I'll go out the front door and get the dogs."

I sat up in bed and heard my dad gently closing the screen door, then a low whistle, then silence. Mom peeked her head into my room and said, "Go back to sleep, baby. Your dad's just checking on the dogs."

Right as she finished saying this the dogs went ballistic. I could hear them scratching at the bricks of the house and snapping the branches of the azaleas. Above their growling, my dad let loose a wild yell punctuated by the sharp crack of his pistol.

Brandy, who woke up with a yelp at the sound of the gun, huddling close to me and clutching my arm. Keen burst in and received sharp orders from Mom to stay with the two of us before she ran to the phone in the living room.

There were differing pitches in the chorus of dogs then, as new animals and people joined in the melee. I could see the beams of flashlights all over the backyard as our neighbors came running down the hill to investigate. A few minutes later the sound of sirens could be heard drawing nearer. When the police arrived, we looked at each other in the pulsing blue light coming through the window and scrunched closer together on the bed, three scared children with a secret blown wide open.

Any minute the cops would come in to get us. We'd be handcuffed together and shoved into the smoky maroon interior of the Sheriff's squad car. I imagined what people would think in the morning when they saw us kids being driven toward our doom, the county jail. We'd be thrown into adjacent cells and given only bread and water to eat for the rest of our lives. I was a criminal at the age of seven, though I wasn't quite sure what I'd done. It wasn't fair. I was being wrongfully accused and I planned how to make my escape from a life of imprisonment. I thought about giving up the other two in a plea deal—I'd watched too many late-night cop dramas with my dad when I couldn't sleep—but in the end I decided to only rat out Brandy.

The sounds and lights and braying of the dogs continued for some time, but eventually began to fade. We could hear voices outside then, though we were unable to make out the words. One by one the flashlight bearers flickered out into the night, moving toward their respective homes, whistling the command for their dogs to follow suit. At last, the squad car lights were extinguished and the cars themselves disappeared around the corner of the house and down our winding gravel driveway. My dad summoned us to the living room with an imperious yell as we heard the screen door slam behind him.

■ ■ ■

Keen and I sat straight up on the couch in our pajamas, our backs not touching the cushions. Brandy slumped in the recliner, seeming perfectly at ease now that the ordeal was over. The clock above the TV read 2:03 A.M. For a moment I was tempted to swing my feet since they didn't touch the ground, but I thought the better of it. I could hear the murmur of my parents' voices from the kitchen. The water was running and I thought I heard Mom say something like, "Hold still," to my dad.

They emerged a few minutes later. Dad's hand was wrapped in white gauze and Mom held it gingerly in her own. My dad's clothes were covered with specks of lime and smudged with dirt. In the lamplight they both looked stern. "So why exactly did you shove a box of junk under the house?" Dad asked.

"It's a time capsule," Keen said.

"Oh, for goodness sake. Now it's scattered all over the backyard. Possums got into it," Mom said.

"Whoa, how many were there?" Brandy asked.

"A whole family of them," my dad said. "At least eight, and some rats too, I believe. I swear I saw some more sets of eyes out in the yard before the dogs ran them off."

"It wasn't our idea," I said, refusing to look in Brandy's direction.

"Whose was it, then?" Mom asked. She exchanged a glance with my dad, seemed to make a decision, and then said, "Well, I guess it doesn't really matter."

"You're going to clean up the mess in the morning. And no more going under the house," my dad said as he put his

Before I fell asleep I heard Mom laugh, a sound I didn't know I'd missed until just then.

arm around Mom and drew her to his side. "Now you all go back to bed."

Keen and I looked at each other with eyes wide with shock at getting off so easily, but we didn't want to push it. We leapt up from the couch, said a hasty goodnight, and scurried back toward our dens. Once I was safely in the hallway I paused for moment to look behind me, expecting to see one or both parents staring me down to make sure I actually went to bed. Instead I saw my mom pull my dad over toward the couch. She grabbed the TV remote off the coffee table on the way and then they sat down. He rested his uninjured arm around her shoulders, and I headed back to my room. Before I fell asleep I heard Mom laugh, a sound I didn't know I'd missed until just then.

■ ■ ■

When I woke up late the next morning it was snowing. Brandy was gone, probably picked up early by her parents' housekeeper. The glass of my bedroom window was cool to the touch and the flurries outside were dropping a powder-fine coat over our backyard. Dad stood in the backyard in his green coat, waiting for the dogs to finish their business. They sniffed at shredded cardboard and one of them crunched on a piece of a chew toy. I saw no trace of the doll.

When I checked, Mom's gold Ford Taurus wasn't in the driveway, so I figured she was at work. I went into the kitchen and saw Keen eating a bowl of Cocoa Puffs at the kitchen table. He nodded toward something in the middle of the table with a look of loathing, so I moved closer to check it out. Beside a vase of fresh sunflowers sat a list of chores with our names written at the top.

I sat down at the table and grabbed the Corn Flakes, pouring them into my plastic Disney Pocahontas bowl. As I sloshed milk over the flakes I thought about Brandy at the mall, picking out a new doll to replace the one she'd lost while her mother admired herself in the glass windows of the store. I sprinkled a generous tablespoon full of brown sugar into my bowl and looked into the future as I did so, seeing Brandy at middle age. She looked exactly like her mother, sitting at brunch with her friends and laughing that cheery, false laugh I guessed rich women were supposed to learn. My mom's laugh didn't sound like that. I hoped mine never would either.

My brother continued his attack on his cereal, only pausing to scowl when he bit his tongue. He took a long gulp of apple juice and continued. I imagined who he would be: taller than our dad, I thought, and maybe his hair would finally decide whether it was blond or brown, but the farthest into his future that I could see was high school. He would play baseball, or basketball, or run track, or maybe even join the swim team. He might start a band. He would be the person everyone knew. The teachers would like him too, and the coaches, and the bus drivers. Beyond his graduation speech, Keen's future dropped off the edge of my imagination.

As for me, I had no idea what my life would look like at all. I chased the last few soggy pieces of cereal around my bowl with my spoon while I tried on professions in my head. I would be a receptionist like Mom, typing away at a keyboard and answering phones with polite, curt tones. I would be a construction worker for Duval & Sons. I would be an Olympic athlete, and my balance beam routine would earn me a gold medal. I would be a fighter pilot like my dad had dreamed of, and when I flew by people would rush out of their houses to see me swirl and spiral through the air. I would be an archeologist, and spend my days in faraway countries, digging, digging, digging, out in the sun or in dark caves. I slurped the last of last of my sugar-filled milk and assumed my profession for that day: housemaid.

■ ■ ■

I probably wouldn't have gone out to the shed for several days, but when I couldn't find the old broom we used to sweep the porch, Dad suggested I check the shed. So I squelched through the already melting snow in my green rain boots to search for it. I stopped outside to stamp the mud off my shoes and then shoved the door open. The broom was propped against the far wall and I marched back to grab it, noticing that the crowbar was back in its usual place and that the paint cans on the lower shelf had been rearranged. I felt a pulse of fear for my secret objects and knelt down to find them. Propped up with my little yarn balls sitting in her lap was the doll. He curls were frizzed and her dress had some dirt stains, but she was all in one piece, and she was all mine. ■

MY FOUR POLE CREEK

Your sources are three:
Clouds, me, and
how the sun likes to

see your dogwoods
glowing white and pink and
your catalpa trees,

too, which insist
on the flurry of their butter-
yellow eaves.

Yet you are never
more yourself than
when you are making your

self over for me—
a roiling brown cloth
torn by a wind that screams

or roughed-up by
green-haunted fall leaves,
the bounty of thunder.

LLEWELLYN McKERNAN

IN FOUR POLE

floats a bowl of light, then
thick-as-gum silver wrinkles the creek, and

now the sun lays brush fires that
flame, arc and leap from the surface—

their sweeping glare blinds
the eyes of heaven, and mine get relief

only from the shade's
good deeds, lingering bank-wise at the

water's small feet: here
lies the latticed ticking of a willow's

shadow, there the
black crux of a crow, everywhere

the seductive
sound of high indigo notes plucked from

a fiddle, filling
 the water with its immeasurable music.

LLEWELLYN McKERNAN

SUBMITTING
POETRY TO
LITERARY JOURNALS

MARIANNE WORTHINGTON

R ecently writer Dheepa Maturi
shared the anguish she
experienced in submitting work
to literary journals. On *Brevity Magazine*'s
nonfiction blog she says, "Each rejection
[I received] felt personal, visceral, like a
judgment rendered upon me...I wanted
to hold each editor by the shoulders and
explain what each line, each sentence

meant. Eventually, I had to accept that my words might be disliked, brutally misinterpreted, or not understood at all, yet they needed to be released to the universe anyway. Slowly, I have come to understand. *To submit* is not necessarily to surrender, tasting dust and defeat. Rather, it is an offering of one's own particular concoction of shame and valor and pain and insight to others, as an act of love."

Whether you have a little or a lot of experience submitting your work to literary journals, the truth is our work is rejected more often than it is accepted. In addition to being a poet myself, I serve as poetry editor at *Still: The Journal*, and I often think about why it's important for us as writers to keep writing and to keep submitting our work.

I helped to establish *Still* in 2009 because my co-founders and I wanted writers from the Appalachian region and beyond to have an online home with us. We strive to give space to writers from a particular region that we feel is underrepresented on the national scene largely due to prejudice about our region. The wealth of literary talent in Appalachia is pervasive and vast, and we want those voices to be heard.

At the same time, we want to broaden the definitions of what rural writing or working class writing or Appalachian writing is. We want diversity in voice and form. We want work about our region, representative of our Appalachian culture—but we also want work that transcends place, becomes something greater than its subject. We like work that is layered and complex, that is smart, and wildly imaginative and that promises some sort of transformation beyond the words on a page. We are especially partial to work that swerves away from the expected—especially those stereotypical notions or prejudices people often hold about Appalachia. You know the ones: granny sitting on the porch of her cabin smoking a corncob pipe, or the feuding hillbilly shooting at revenuers and his neighbors, or the beautiful but ignorant wood nymph that is "saved" by the outsider, or the noble Cherokee savage, or the Trump supporter representing an entire region of people, etc., etc., etc.

Often when we read work submitted to *Still: The Journal* we find that the submitters have not paid attention to our mission statement. We find that submitters have probably never looked at a past issue of *Still*. The first order of business, then, is to read and research journals that might be a good fit with your work. Read carefully past issues of those journals to see if your work is in line with what those journals accept. If not, keep researching and reading. I tell my students every day that reading widely helps us be better writers. They often are resistant. They don't believe me, and sometimes they take any sort of critical feedback about their writing as a personal assault, just like Dheepa Maturi did.

Once you find some journals that you think would accept your work, work diligently to observe the stated submission guidelines. Read the directions for correctly formatting and submitting your work. Editors spend a lot of energy writing and refining their submission guidelines. For instance, we recently revamped how we prefer submitters to write their biographical note. We found that so many people write the most outrageous biographies. Here are some actual examples we've received:

"I was raised by wolves and vultures."

"Once upon a time a girl was born to parents who didn't know how to love her."

"I am quaint. I have hippy blood. Ain't it cool?"

When we received these actual biographies, we knew it was time to revisit our guidelines. These examples and other extreme biographical statements not only seem like desperate attention grabbers but also have nothing to do with writing and are offputting to most editors.

We also pay attention to vivid voice and to intricate language in poetry. If your poetry does not have a single image or a metaphor or a simile; if it does not show any use of craft or music, if the poem is not marked by the pleasing or surprising use of the line or syntax or diction, then we think your poem is probably not yet ready to meet the reader. We are always looking for poems that know what they are doing.

We also consider how much care the writer has taken in revision and editing. For me, a deal breaker is a submission riddled with typos, grammar errors, spelling errors. I feel the submitter has disrespected our journal and me as poetry editor, and I don't take the writer seriously.

My heart often breaks when I reject writers' work. However, with each rejection, I think we become stronger writers. For instance, I had been sending around one particular poem for over a year. And every place I sent it, rejected it. I'd probably sent it to over a dozen journals. So, I took the poem back. Instead of saying "what is wrong with these stupid editors who won't publish my poem?" I finally was able to say, "what is wrong with this poem?" I probably spent six months revising that poem. I sent it out again, and the first place I sent it, took the poem.

I had to learn, like Dheepa Maturi and all of us, that rejection is not "necessarily to surrender, tasting dust and defeat." But with careful revision, the poem became "an act of love." ■

SUBURBAN ORCHESTRAL

Tulips, glass rabbits, and little moons,
scratched and shivered, their braille messages
unreadable constellations under my fingertips.
Refrigerator cold exhaled against the dish,
dropped dyes swimming smoke-like in a vinegar pool.

Sanity walks a tightrope.
Snow-crunch of exam table paper, and the needles
lips into my hand, suave as a dance partner.
Daffodils know to hold back
for the opportune moment.

I want to be *believed*—
and this year, I won't mistake
the iris leaves for weeds.
I will right the toppled bricks
the rain-soaked soil has heaved.

NATALIE HOMER

DRIVING THROUGH

safe car on safe road and highway switchbacks
baby girl with those gray wristbands on
plastic pellet resting between tendons
keeping her stomach still or at least stiller

than the black car and its sticky summer seats
tight gridlines on the backs of our thighs
little white house peeking up at her
from below the grey metal guardrails

little creek smaller than the river she knows
playing peekaboo with the swaying road
carved strip in the mountain on the other side
she knows the word *logging* thanks to

Richard Scarry's overall'd cat-boy
but maybe he's a girl like her who didn't
know the dirt turns such a yellow-red color
when they take the trees away

and string those wires along like
a tree-lined set of hand-over-hand bars
and it's still light out and they haven't
stopped for lunch and her brother

wonders where the mountain's trees went
and wonders where all the houses' people are
while his mom looks out the window and
says how beautiful it is along that road

and her voice sounds like a book's end
that he doesn't understand and he'd like
to play in the creek he keeps seeing but
they don't stop till the houses are gone

when the bracelets stop working
because the road is just like his sister's
belly and nothing like that stays still
when they have other places to go

EMMA APRILE

OCCUPATIONAL THERAPY

The morning's pain pill weighs her
down. Unseen winter birds ask her
to remember
spring. She   cannot recognize their calls.
She postpones her pill   as long as her coffee lasts.
The pin inside her arm conducts weather to her bones, but she doesn't know why.
Yesterday's paper unfolds across her table. A miniature blue motorcycle's plastic parts
cover Jerusalem's riots, & paints smear over tax cuts, advertisements: reports on a world
that's come & gone while she slept. Wool-blanket sky shrouds her bedroom. No one could
tell the time with their sun buried in clouds.   She has come to hate nature's moody
reflections. Before the accident, her hours   opened like highways, but today crumples,
slices its light through thin shutters, obscures   its own horizon. Instructions fold themselves into an origami bird, & she's confined to hidden routes insides its square stomach, along the creased & recreased
folds of its triangular wings. Each pill's white circle cushions her in cotton, cradles her elbow's splintered bones inside
its haze. The model's tiniest parts hop   away across the news. Words she used
to use—conflict, interior, accord—now   difficult to define. Alone, she folds
her scars into her chest. Cold,   damp, easily torn: the model's
instructions test dexterity.   She stares at her loosened
skin, waiting for her   muscles, pink & striated
behind their casings, to unfold, to open like a pair of wings—if only she could remember what for.

EMMA APRILE

GOODBYE
ALICE

KIM SHEGOG

H er shoes are shiny, her dress is not yet wrinkled, and her bangs are still secured by a tortoise shell clip. She stands in front of the television watching cartoons. Kate stands because she listens to her mother: prevent wrinkles—no sitting until the car ride.

She hears her sister walking up the hall in her high heels. Did she see the pink, heart-shaped stickers stuck to the soles? Kate doesn't know for sure, but just because she isn't allowed to wear heels yet doesn't mean she isn't allowed to touch them.

Her sister calls for their mother. Kate listens. It's about accessories. It nearly always was. She could never find this purse or those earrings or a matching scarf. This time it's the purse. She can't find the small, black leather bag with the strap that looks like gold paper clips hooked together. Of course she couldn't find it. It's hanging on Kate's shoulder. There are things Kate needs to carry, too. Her shell-shaped mirror, strawberry lip-gloss, and purple velvet change purse, she has to carry those things. Now was not the time to jam them into her backpack. She needs something dressy and grown up. This purse, swiped from her sister's closet, is perfect.

People would see her at Rolling Acres Christian Church, and they need to know she belongs.

She'd heard her mother and sister talking last night in the kitchen. They'd assumed Kate was in bed, but she was really hiding in the living room, listening through the wall. At only seven, she'd learned to press one ear to the wall so she'd hear what was happening on the other side. It didn't take her long to discover the most interesting conversations occurred when people thought she was sleeping.

Like the time she heard her father explain how the neighbor's son, Darryl, lit his mother's cat on fire. Kate's mother shouted "Oh, my Lord," followed by a rant of questions about why somebody hadn't done something for Darryl's mental condition. After all, he'd set a section of his parent's backyard on fire last summer. The flames jumped the shared driveway, but Kate's father'd been home, saving the day with the garden hose.

Kate wasn't too upset about the cat. He'd scratched her face once when she'd tried to stuff his face in a bowl of milk. The cats on TV always drank milk.

Her mother said something about Mrs. Shirley's daughter, Alice, and a funeral. Mrs. Shirley, a member of their church, was Kate's Sunday school teacher last year. To her, Kate was "just the best little thing" in class. Never put up a fuss about anything. Walked in and sat at the table with her children's Bible and a smile on her face. Even though she wasn't Kate's teacher anymore, she'd give her peppermints on Sunday mornings. Kate didn't realize Mrs. Shirley was a mother. She was just the nice old lady with the candy.

"Of course your sister's going with us," she'd heard her mother say. After that, their words came too fast through the wall for Kate to keep up.

Her sister marches into the den, smashing papers and tubes of lipstick in a shiny silver clutch. She throws the bag on the couch and walks behind Kate to get a magazine from the coffee table.

Lately, she's been too mature to watch cartoons with her little sister. She insists on flipping through the pages of magazines like those women on television—the sophisticated women with cemented hairdos and flawless faces, the ones who'd have an "after dinner drink" with their husbands. She'd been Lizzy for the past sixteen years, but she now refuses to answer to anything other than Elizabeth. Except when Kate calls her *Eliza-death*. She always responds to her sister then.

The pressure of her stare burns through Kate's wool dress and into her back. Kate's cheeks flush hot. She knew Elizabeth had seen the purse on her shoulder, but she keeps her eyes fixed on the bears dancing on the screen. They are wearing bright pink tutus and ballet slippers.

"If we weren't getting ready to leave, and I didn't think Mom would make me put you back together again, I would smack you to the ground," Elizabeth says, turning one shiny page after the other.

Kate doesn't open her mouth. Their mother appears from the hall. Both girls are glad to see her for different reasons.

"Let's put on your coats," she says.

Their mother, in a black dress with a simple strand of pearls clinging to her neck, should be on television. Not one loose hair or a piece of lint anywhere. Women compliment her often, as if they'd almost forgotten, or forgiven, where she came from.

Before she was a wife, Elizabeth's mother and then Kate's mother, she had been Sandra Lane, daughter to an adulterer who abandoned his family for his employer's younger sister. The event didn't cause Sandra's mother to lose her mind because it was mostly gone already, but it did make Sandra's life worse. Her mother became more suspicious of women, including her daughter, forbidding her to wear anything other than oversized denim pants and sweaters. No cosmetics or hair treatments, sneakers only, and no dentist appointment to repair a chipped front tooth. It was a wonder, a miracle really, she was saved by Kate's father in high school. Everybody said so. They'd married three weeks after graduation, after he'd paid for her to have her tooth fixed. She was a nice enough girl, and fell on hard times for sure, but what he, a handsome young man with a bright future, saw in her, people couldn't put a name to. He must've been an angel put on Earth just for her.

Her mother pulls a small but heavy, black wool coat from a hanger in the closet. Kate removes the purse strap from her shoulder and sits the bag by her foot.

"You are not taking it," her mother says, buttoning Kate's coat to the top, choking her into fashion. "It's not appropriate for a little girl to carry a woman's purse."

She looks at her daughter, and Kate, not turning away, squeezes out a tear.

"Well, you can take the purse in the car, but you'd better leave it there when we get out," her mother says. She turns the television off with the remote control, and an attractive woman evaluating her two daughters is reflected in the dark glass.

One tiny tear was all it'd take. Kate knew how to handle her mother to get what she wanted.

Although she'd never been to a funeral before, she'd seen one on television. She remembered seeing only grown-ups, and they all looked sad. Some of them cried. Her mother must've considered her a grown-up, too.

It's a long ride to Kate, so she feels has enough time to validate her belongings. She unzips the bag and removes her change purse. The purple velvet so beautiful and soft, she rubs her fingers over it then shakes it. She knows the contents: three quarters, four dimes, and two pennies. The quarters came from her mother as payment for cleaning her closet, she found the dimes under the cushion in her father's recliner, and the two pennies were change from her lip-gloss purchase. She pulls out the lip-gloss,

One tiny tear was all it'd take. Kate knew how to handle her mother to get what she wanted.

unscrews the top, and brings the tube close to her nose. The scent of strawberry candy and make-up is exciting. She rubs the sticky mixture over her lips, smacking them together, the way she'd seen her mother do when she applied her coral red lipstick. She digs the shell-shaped mirror from the purse. Perfect.

Kate knew when they'd arrived at the church by the way her mother turned into the parking lot. She'd use her left hand to flip the sun visor up and into its place while her right hand rotated the steering wheel. Then she would mash the gas pedal, and their Volvo charged up the hill. Kate loved that part of the ride.

The front parking lot is full, so they drive around the back of the church where the cemetery is. Kate sees something that looks like a tent standing between some of the graves. The cemetery was the best place for hide and go seek. On Wednesday nights, if the family made it to church, Kate and her friends played back there. Not really allowed, but the grownups didn't say no until chubby Kevin Clayton tripped in a mole's hole and knocked out one of his front teeth on somebody's stone. He squalled like a baby, his mother went crazy, and Kate's father said no more games in the cemetery.

Kate's father owns Ramsey Volvo and Used Cars. When he travels to view new models or pick up a used car, he brings home gifts for his girls, including his wife. Sometimes he'll call her "his girl," which makes Elizabeth gag and Kate smile. The last time he went on a business trip, he returned with a talking doll for Kate. Her name was Misty, and Kate loved her until the batteries went dead, and her mother kept forgetting to buy more when she went grocery shopping. Misty now resides face down under Kate's bed with an empty gumball machine and her sister's old pogo stick.

He's in Chicago, but he'll be home in three days. He calls every night to talk to his wife. He asks to speak to Kate, but she doesn't like to talk on the phone. It makes her sad to hear his voice so far away. Elizabeth refuses to speak to him on the grounds he's keeping the current love of her life from getting through.

Their mother finds a space, parks the car, and turns to her daughters. Examining Elizabeth first, she plucks a few strands of brown hair from her coat. Kate, always in the back seat, requires no further attention at the moment.

"Be very quiet when we go inside. Don't speak unless spoken to," their mother says, her eyes focused on her youngest. Kate's cheeks burn red again, frustrated and embarrassed at her mother's refusal to recognize her transformation today.

As they get out, Kate sees more and more cars pulling in. No sounds of talking or laughter as others join in the walk to the entrance. The air is stinging cold. Some women are draped in thick furs like Kate's mother in her chestnut mink. Men keep their hands tucked into their coat pockets until they reach the door where they grasp the cold brass handle to usher in the ladies. Kate notices there is no Sunday bell. Mr. Yardley always rang the bell at church. One time he even allowed Kate into the bell tower to see how it worked. She bragged about the experience to her friends at her private school. They weren't impressed.

Kate fails to recognize many of the people surrounding her. Not one person is smiling. She shuffles to her mother's side to wedge herself between her and her sister. Here, she'll be safe. Her mother clasps her hand as they reach the door. Kate hears her sister's high heels clap and clunk as she walks across the brass doorframe and onto the tile. They fumble in the doorway, removing coats and placing them on the wooden hangers. Elizabeth touches her earlobes, reassured her diamond studs are still in place. Kate's mother whisks her hands over her dress first, then Kate's, taking her hand again. As they walk through the foyer, Kate's mother speaks in a low, soft voice to the men and women milling about. Elizabeth offers a few words.

Mrs. Shirley shuffles toward Kate, a white lace handkerchief wrapped around her fingers. Her face, red and puffy, reminds Kate of Elizabeth when her boyfriend broke up with her last week. She'd collapsed on her bed after the tragedy, sobbing and flailing on the bedspread. Kate brought a cool washcloth into her room, and her sister rolled over, jerked it from her hand, yelling, "Leave me alone."

Kneeling in front of Kate, Mrs. Shirley kisses her cheek. "She's the prettiest little thing," she says. "Both of your girls. Pretty." Her husband, gripping her hand, pulls her up, and they back away. Kate, wanting to speak, raises her eyes toward her mother, but she shakes her head no, pulling Kate through the foyer with Elizabeth following. Their mother stops at a tall pedestal, writing all three names in perfect script. After taking a folded piece of paper from the surface, they walk inside the sanctuary.

They creep along with the rest, a silent line of lowered heads. Kate's mother holds her hand as they shuffle to the altar. Kate stares at the lady's back in front of her. Her dress is navy blue with tan stripes. Her legs, much bigger than Kate's mother's, are wrapped in dark pantyhose, her large feet crammed in dark blue shoes. A long, curly string dangles from the bottom of her dress. Kate reaches to tear it off, as she'd seen her mother do many times, but her mother squeezes her hand.

A long, shiny casket lay before them with a young woman's body tucked inside. She wears a lavender dress with a high lace collar and ruffles on her sleeves. Kate wonders if the lace is choking her.

"See the high neckline?" Elizabeth leans forward and whispers into Kate's ear. "It's to cover up the rope marks. Mom heard Alice hanged herself from the ceiling fan in her dorm room."

Elizabeth disappears behind and returns her stare to the toe of her shoes while Kate's eyes focus on Alice. Their mother sniffles, but Kate doesn't look up. Her little chest brushes the casket's edge as she leans closer.

The young woman's face, a glowing white, has red circles painted on her cheeks and purple eye shadow on her lids. Kate's gaze moves down the body, stopping at the young woman's hands. Her right hand, resting on top of her left, is milky white with dark purple lines crossing underneath the skin. Her fingernails, painted a pale pink, make Kate wish for the color herself. She wants to reach inside the casket and feel, touch a dead hand. She strains her neck to the side, attempting a look farther into the casket to see the girl's legs, but they're hidden in the dark. Kate's mother squeezes her hand, using more pressure this time, moving them away from Alice.

They join the line of others, extending handshakes and somber hugs to the family standing by Alice. Men and women on both sides of the line are crying. Some weep loud and gasp for air, hiccupping with open mouths.

Mrs. Shirley, shoulders hunched and trembling, nods her head. Kate offers her small hand like the others, but Mrs. Shirley fails to take hold. She leaves her arm extended until Elizabeth pushes her forward. "Just go on," she says, her fingernail digging into Kate's back.

At the end of the line, their mother ushers her daughters to a back pew. Before sitting, she smiles, mouth closed, the flawed tooth haunting her, and whispers, "Chicago" to a man and his wife nearby.

No Mr. Betram, their regular pastor, no lady to play the organ, no choir in blue robes with red sashes. Kate's church is unrecognizable. Her mother reads the paper from the pedestal like it's one of her romance novels, only inches from her nose while she mouths the words. Kate stares at her sister as she digs in her purse, wishing she could do the same—the taste of her strawberry lip gloss long gone by now. Kate takes a Bible and Prayer Request card from the back of the pew in front her. She taps her sister's arm, pointing to a pencil near her, which she tosses to Kate after an impressive eye roll.

She needed answers to some important questions. She'd see Mr. Bertram tomorrow morning, so now was a good time to make her list.

1. What do people wear in Heaven?
2. Will I have my own room?
3. Is there television?

Her mother takes the Bible from Kate's lap as she finishes writing her last and most important question. Kate folds the card into a small square and presents it to her mother, who places it inside her purse.

A man's voice booms from the podium. He's the young pastor from the university chapel.

As he speaks, women sniffle, and a man toward the front has a coughing fit. Kate's mother nods as the pastor offers enthusiastic words of consolation and explanation. Elizabeth picks at her dry cuticles while Kate thumps her shoe on the tile, her toes tingling and burning from lack of movement. Her mother, horrified, looks at her with wild eyes and pinches the back of her arm. Kate scoots her back against the pew, crossing her legs at the ankles like a good girl, and rests her hands in her lap.

After claiming a final "Amen," the young pastor invites everyone to follow him outside.

He strides down the center aisle, his black robe unzipped and flowing, exposing his tie, navy blue with a scarlet cross in its center with rays of fairer scarlet bursting forth. Like a vision in a dream, out of focus, but the colors radiant and swirling, he secures the gaze of all attendees.

Kate climbs onto the pew cushion, hoping for a clearer view, but her mother catches her, ordering her down with the stare of her pale blue eyes. As the casket passes by their row, the three of them exit the pew and join the procession of others shuffling their way outside. The mourners stand, circling the dark green tent, the chairs underneath filled with those who knew Alice best or loved her most or both.

Mrs. Shirley faces the casket. Kate wonders how long this part is going to take.

Outside is still cold, the temperature having dropped a few degrees since the service began. Nobody'd thought to retrieve a coat from the foyer, or maybe they decided it was unacceptable to leave the crowd. Kate shivers, clinging to her mother's hand. Her mother'd taken hold of it as they walked. Soothed, Kate grinned and interlaced her fingers with her mother's. She'd been forgiven for her earlier offenses.

The young pastor raises his hands into the air, palms up. He invites those gathered to bow their heads. He prays, open eyed, for "everlasting peace" for Alice and her loved ones. To Kate, his voice seems angry, and he uses too many big words, making her thankful for Mr. Bertram's gentle way.

Then it is over. Everyone's duty fulfilled, they begin to walk away. Back to their cars to begin their own lives again, moving past this brief disruption.

Kate notices more chatter as people move toward their cars, some forming small groups.

She hears lunch plans and sees toothy grins. Some of the women brag about what dish they'd taken to the Shirleys.

She hears another someone ask her mother why her "good-looking husband" hadn't been with them. She explains he was out of town on business.

Then it is over. Everyone's duty fulfilled, they begin to walk away. Back to their cars to begin their own lives again, moving past this brief disruption.

Kate wishes he'd been with them, especially when they were in the cemetery. He'd have wrapped the edge of his suit coat around her to keep her warm. He'd do things like that for her sometimes.

Their mother unlocks the car, and they climb inside. Elizabeth, who'd been instructed to retrieve the coats, throws them in the back seat, burying Kate underneath the pile. Kate digs her way out and reaches for her purse. She opens the shell-shaped mirror to evaluate her face. Her droopy eyes mean she needs a nap, but otherwise she'd held together well.

Elizabeth and her mother talk all the way home. They discuss the service, the people, the clothes, and the weather. Kate, fading in and out of consciousness, is not invited into their conversation. Instead, she sits with her head relaxed to the side, catching a few glimpses of the outside:

An old lady still in her housecoat walking from her mailbox with nothing in her hands.

Mrs. Shirley was rude to me today when she didn't shake my hand like she did everyone else.

A buzzard picks at a dead animal's guts on the side of the road.

Can worms and bugs dig through the casket and get to Alice?

Mr. Lawson's cows standing in the field.

Daddy never did take me to visit the farm like he promised.

When Kate hears the sound of the garage door rising, she's reenergized. She runs into the house, tosses her sister's purse on the kitchen counter, missing the porcelain fruit bowl by an inch. She'll retrieve her belongings later when she's looking for something to do.

In her room, she pulls off her dress and tights, piling them on the floor.

Her mother walks in her room. "Hang up your dress and fold your tights and put them in your drawer," she says.

Kate huffs as her mother walks out of the room, but she does as she instructed because she listens to her mother.

As she stretches the neck of her dress around the hanger, she can't stop thinking about Alice. She wonders if her mother would make her wear that kind of dress when she dies, an itchy looking one with a high collar. She'd have to ask her sometime.

The phone rings. Kate's mother brings her the cordless. It's her father, wanting to talk to her like always, and today, she returns his favor.

"Hey, Daddy. How many more days until you come home?" she asks, walking in a circle around the blue edge of her rainbow colored rug.

"Shortcake," he says. "Be there before you know it. What can I bring you? You know, something little, so as not to spoil you too much." He joked about spoiling his girls, especially Kate since she was the baby.

"I saw the prettiest pink nail polish today, daddy. Can you bring me some?" Kate says.

"How about I take you with me to get some when I get home? To make sure we get the right one?" he says.

"Okay. I'll tell you all about it," Kate says. "Love you." She gives the phone to her mother, leaning against the doorframe. She takes over the conversation as she walks up the hall.

Kate stands in front of her dresser, making faces in the mirror. A toothy grin, a frown, a mad face—all the faces her mother claims are ugly and asks her, "What would you do if your face froze that way?"

Climbing onto her bed, she lies on her stomach and tucks her arms underneath her pillow. She releases a tight yawn, closing her eyes. The voices of her mother and sister carry down the hall and into her room. Their words surround her, covering her like a bandage. Today she's been a child and a young woman and it's been exhausting, so she sleeps. The best kind, deep, peaceful, and pure. Second only to a permanent sleep, like Alice's. ∎

BOOK REVIEWS

Savannah Sipple. *WWJD and Other Poems*. Little Rock, Ar.: Sibling Rivalry Press, 2019. 74 pages. Softcover. $15.95.

Reviewed by Jessica Cory

Savannah Sipple's debut poetry collection *WWJD and Other Poems* is a manifesto of self-acceptance, self-love, and the difficult passage in embodying these notions amid a society that conditions us to feel shame about who we are. But make no mistake, this collection isn't all feel-good inspiration. While there are plenty of beautiful and hilarious moments throughout *WWJD and Other Poems*, Sipple includes plenty of middle fingers and heartbreak to balance them out. From domestic abuse and toxic masculinity to church  on Sunday and mountaintop removal, this collection engages with the complexities of the region and the self while still maintaining a strong authorial voice that's wholly queer, Appalachian, and unapologetic.

From a technical standpoint, one of the details that strikes me about Sipple's collection is her obvious attention to line integrity. She uses line breaks and spacing in a very determined way in order to create specific (or a multitude of) meanings. Sipple also utilizes a variety of forms, such as a BINGO board for "EVANGELISM BINGO" and a numbered list in "A List of Times I Thought I was Gay" to literally queer how readers visually identify poetry, stretching the boundaries that decide what shapes the genre can take.

Sipple expands the boundaries of the Appalachian imagination throughout her poems' content as well by unabashedly embracing rural queerness. These aren't poems about the queer urban experience, and it's this precise difference from which the poems derive their power. There are guns, trucks, four-wheelers, and cheap beer. There are soup beans and green beans and fatback. By using the imagery of her surroundings, Sipple is providing ever-important representation to the rural queer experience. She's saying "girls who like girls don't just exist in NYC and Atlanta and on TV. We're at the local IGA. We're your next door neighbors canning peaches." This collection does focus on self-discovery, however, and Sipple's speaker refuses to shy away from the struggle of realizing she's queer, as the opening poem, "I Wanted You To Fuck Me," ends with a pleading: "*please* bang me straight" (15). As the collection progresses, though, we see the speaker step into her truth by engaging in erotic moments with women and no longer denying her own identity.

Sipple furthers the queer rural identity through her use of dialect, rooting the poems in a regional place. In "Cant," for example, the speaker notes that "Men call girls sis here, women too, / even when they want to fuck them," a pronoun usage most folks in Appalachia are quite familiar with. Additionally, phrases like "You take what you want / from me, say you're full as a tick burrowed in a hound" (33) and "I couldn't give a rat's ass about lures" (39) locate the collection in a rural environment that, evidenced by their usage, shows how proud the speaker is of her home region and how determined she is to remain within its space.

In addition to exploring queer rural identity, this collection also serves as a cultural critique, rejecting the fat-shaming that's constantly on parade in contemporary American society. Sipple's poems illustrate the binaries of self-hatred and self-love of the body. Sometimes the speaker is celebrating: "Pass whole milk, pass the milk fat; pass chocolate, also bad for my face; pass brie" (37), seeing her body as "sycamore solid" (30), and exploring the ways in which "boxing makes me feel beautiful because muscles contract under my / backfat ripples" (37). Other moments in these poems are much more stark, such as when the speaker recalls her seventeenth birthday: "the end of a liquid diet, I celebrated / with a baked potato, no sour cream, no butter" as her mother warned *"Be careful so / you don't gain back the fat"* (37). These juxtapositions work to not only maintain the speaker's identity as a complex human with her own struggles rather than simply a figurehead for the fat acceptance movement, but they also implicate people who contribute to these biases, even if they're the speaker's own kin or larger systems at work, such as patriarchy and the toxic masculinity that it can produce.

WWJD asks its readers to bear witness to the realities created by toxic masculinity, as the speaker works to reconcile with the experiences she holds while not necessarily reconciling with the offenders. Readers serve as bystanders while the speaker struggles to create a sense of home that exists without the abuse she suffered at the hand of a father who "claimed he'd knock my goddamn head off" when the speaker "was nine" (30) and as she tries to simply exist as female in a place where "They rut young girls" (19). The reimagining of Jesus and religion plays a significant role in the speaker's understanding of these circumstances, as we see in "WWJD / on prayer," that "Jesus would stop talking to my father / who last threatened / to hit me when I was six / no twelve / no twenty-six" (54). As religious interpretations have long been utilized to oppress and control women, the speaker's choice to turn to her relationship with Christ as a way to process difficult situations speaks to way in which Sipple both implicates and brilliantly reimagines religion in *WWJD*.

Part III of the collection is centered on the title's question that we often see emblazoned on rubber wristbands and across chrome bumpers: What Would Jesus Do? Except that Sipple's Jesus is more human than the one we learned of in Sunday school. He's more *Dogma*'s Buddy Christ than crucifix, and his humanity is exactly what makes him divine. The message that Sipple conveys through Christ's corporeality is that the human body, and we as humans, are divine and we should revel in our identities and our physical forms, even if we (or society) deem them imperfect. This philosophy is perfectly captured in "Jesus shouts, *Amen!*" when the speaker finally realizes that "My body is a holler I've tried to escape / time and again, but now, with this woman, I am home" (64) and is echoed in the understanding that "You don't / have to image you're male. You don't need / a dick to be loved" (65). As the speaker reconciles her identity, we see her locate comfort and happiness, notes on which the collection closes. In the final poem, "[Jesus rides shotgun]," we see Jesus and the speaker enjoying a reckless joyride, as the speaker admits, "I used to be afraid. Sometimes / I still am. Maybe." and Jesus advises from the passenger seat, *"Don't hit the brakes,... / Turn the wheel. That's how you know / the way you want to go"* (66). This divine encouragement to move forward despite the speaker's anxieties seems to summarize what the speaker has learned throughout her journey thus far: that no matter how difficult life is, plowing ahead is the only way things will get better, a sentiment that as readers, we can also appreciate, having been along for the ride.

Natalie Sypolt. *The Sound of Holding Your Breath.* Morgantown, W.Va.: West Virginia University Press, 2018. 156 pages. Softcover. $18.99.

Reviewed by Emily Masters

Natalie Sypolt's debut collection of short stories, *The Sound of Holding Your Breath*, is full of characters and moments that will stay with readers long after they lay down the book. The fourteen stories in this collection feature characters who struggle to find who they are, to wrestle with grief and disaster, who hit rock bottom and sometimes can't find a way to claw their way back up. Sypolt, who has had many of her stories published in *Appalachian Heritage, Kestrel, Still: The Journal*, and other journals, includes two new stories in this collection: "Ghosts" and "Wanting Baby."

The Sound of Holding Your Breath should come with a warning that readers will not want to put the book down once they crack the spine to the first page. "Diving" drops readers right into an Appalachian kitchen, immediately solidifying the sense of place she weaves throughout her stories. The examinations of gender roles and the ways in which a community is dealing with a young boy's death set the grim, yet urgent, tone for the rest of the collection. Although the tone of her collection is dark, Sypolt represents her Appalachian characters in a complex light, developing them fully to make them real.

Sypolt is unafraid to approach the hard parts of life in her stories. Readers will find themselves immersed in stories of death, of murder, of rape, of PTSD, of shame. Readers will, at times, feel like they are drowning, often without any light at the end of the tunnel. Darkness, however, seems to fit Sypolt's writing and voice like a glove, making her characters more relatable and redeemable. Her characters experience situations that would fill anyone with dread. They are gritty and real and pop off the page. After finishing the stories, readers will feel the experiences as if they were lived, not read.

Themes of family, community, fatalism, education, death, and religion are pervasive in the collection. Although her characters do not continue from story to story, they all share the experience of life's most challenging and wrecking events. Characters in the collection love each other in a way that consumes them, leaving behind shells of the people they once were. In "Flaming Jesus," young love ends when one of the characters leaves, unable to confront a life in the same small town under his preacher father's thumb. In the end, he is unable to escape, instead enlisting in the military and flaming out. "Stalking the White Deer" ends in death of a deer, of love, of a positive future for two twin boys who are cursed from birth.

The collection's title story deals with the long-term effects of a childhood rape, and the retaliation as an adult is vindicating. The main character of the story reflects, "Good and bad can be so close together. We all are always brushing up against the line. Evil doesn't exist. The evil thing is just the quick other side of the beautiful thing." In her stories, Sypolt chooses to write about the quick other side of the beautiful thing—a family vacation gone wrong in "At the Lake," the corruption underlying the surface of religion in "Get Up, June," the souring of a relationship after the horrors of war in "Lettuce."

Perhaps the story that best showcases Sypolt's writing talent is "What Would Be Saved." The two-page story reveals her talent for packing in a lot of emotion in few words. Out of the story emerge two characters, husband and wife, who are dynamic and complex. They are indicative of the internal battles we are all fighting and the ways we struggle to cope. The emotion and imagery Sypolt summons in such a brief space is indicative of her talent in the rest of the stories in her debut collection.

If you are looking for stories with happy endings, then *The Sound of Holding Your Breath* is not for you. If, however, you are looking for beautiful writing, haunting images, and a way to embrace the bleakness of the human experience, then you will find yourself at home, skin shivering, in Sypolt's collection. Reading Sypolt's stories is like running through a forest at night, the thorns of her prose catching in the fabric of your memory. The collection is one to read and read again, letting the stories envelop your life, only to be released back into the world, the writing dwelling in the shadowy corners of your mind's attic. ∎

WAFFLE HOUSE, 3 A.M.

We brumble in, early morning dreamers.
I don't know these coffee-thirst folk by name
but I know them, feel their itch and fatigue
in my own bones. We recognize in one another
the lottery win imaginings, the confidence
that comes with a refilled mug running over
on our respective table top kingdoms.
A greasy film on the laminated menu, a fork tine
crusted with dried egg yellow, an escapee
droplet of ketchup from someone's palm heel
banging, a rogue splatter far away from
the consumption of hash browns and sautéed onions.
We came for this. When the new waitress—a local girl
we vaguely remember stacking shelves at the Dollar Store
maybe a month or two ago—when she befuddles, all alone
on the floor with the likes of us mumbling or calling out,
dropping water glasses left and right, everybody laughs
at her expense before scooting out of booths, picking up
shards and tiny diamonds, nodding at one another
knowing we will all tip her large like she's ham gravy
on grits. Drunk teens, old ramblers with no internal clocks,
escapees of the third shift, hard living tweakers attracted
like luna moths to bright lights steaming up
out of nighttime's crust-topped soup. Some need
the large bowl of Bert's Best Bowl of Chili,
smothered covered chucked and peppered;
some even moo while mowing down
Double Angus Cheeseburgers, there's people
shoveling in Papa Joe's pork chops swimming
in mushrooms, onions and cheese, one old dude
is all about sausage biscuits, a sloppy-eyed girl

grins with a mouthful of pecan pie, her face
in two different heavens.
Gathering. Ordering. And if we take our time
the sun comes over the dulled edge of town
a corner occupied by the cemetery and the closed factory
that specialized in a single part for making helicopters spin.
That work now tinkered far across dark water. A few
will solicit others for rides to somewhere close by
when we finally rise, but for now the girl fills our chipped cups
one more time, patient for the crumbs and dollars asleep on
    the tables.

SCOTT HUTCHISON

CONTRIBUTORS

Emma Aprile's poetry has appeared in online and print publications including, most recently, *Shenandoah* and *Antiphon*. She holds an MFA from George Mason University, and works as a copyeditor of literary fiction, nonfiction, and poetry for independent small presses. She lives in Louisville, Kentucky.

Catharina Coenen is a German immigrant to Northwestern Pennsylvania, where she teaches college biology. Her creative non-fiction essays are forthcoming in *5 x 5* and in *The Avalon Literary Review*.

Jessica Cory is a native of southeastern Ohio now residing in western North Carolina where she teaches in the English department at Western Carolina University. Her work has appeared in a variety of journals. She is also the editor of *Where the Sweet Waters Flow: Contemporary Appalachian Nature Writing*, forthcoming from West Virginia University Press.

Cathy Cruise's first novel, *A Hundred Weddings*, was released in December 2016. Her fiction has appeared in journals such as *American Fiction, Michigan Quarterly Review, Blue Mesa Review, New Virginia Review*, and *Phoebe*. Cruise holds an MFA in creative writing from George Mason University and works as an editor in Northern Virginia.

Noah Davis is an MFA candidate at Indiana University and was selected as the 2018 Jean Ritchie Appalachian Literature Fellowship from Lincoln Memorial University. A two-time Pushcart Prize nominee, his poetry has appeared in *North American Review, The Hollins Critic, Atlanta Review, Water~Stone Review*, and *Chautauqua*, and his prose has been published in *Kestrel, Chariton Review, The Fly Fish Journal*, and others.

Natalie Homer is the author of the chapbook *Attic of the Skull* (dancing girl press). Her poetry has been published or is forthcoming in *The Cincinnati Review, The Journal, Cosmonauts Avenue, The Pinch*, *the minnesota review, Blue Earth Review, Ruminate, Salamander, The Lascaux Review, Tinderbox Poetry Journal,* and others. She earned an MFA from West Virginia University and lives in southwestern Pennsylvania.

Scott Hutchison's work has appeared in *The Chattahoochee Review, The Southern Review, The Georgia Review, Kestrel, On the Veranda, Split Rock Review,* and numerous other publications.

Kathleen Brewin Lewis is the author of two chapbooks of poetry, *Fluent in Rivers* and *July's Thick Kingdom.* Her writing has also been published in *Southern Poetry Review, Southern Humanities Review, Tar River Poetry, Cider Press Review,* and *Still: The Journal.*

Bre Lillie is a native of Charlotte, North Carolina. She is currently pursuing an MFA in Creative Writing at the University of Tennessee Knoxville. Her stories and poems have been published in *River and South Review* and *New Limestone Review.* Every July she dons rain boots in defense of rat snakes and picks wild blackberries with her mother on rural side roads.

George Ella Lyon is the former Kentucky Poet Laureate. Her most recent books include *Many-Storied House: Poems, Boats Float!* and *What Forest Knows* (picture books), and *Voices from the March on Washington,* a collection of poetry for young adults co-written with J. Patrick Lewis. A native of Harlan County, Kentucky, she makes her living as a freelance writer and teacher based in Lexington.

Emily Masters is a senior English major at Berea College where she works as a teaching assistant for Silas House and as a student editor of *Appalachian Heritage.* She is from Monteagle, Tennessee, where she lives on a farm with her family. Her work has been published in *Still: The Journal* and *The Pikeville Review.*

Llewellyn McKernan is a poet and teacher who has lived and worked in West Virginia for so long she considers it home. She has a Masters in Creative Writing from Brown University and has been an adjunct English professor at Marshall University, St. Mary's College, and the University of Arkansas. Her published works include six poetry books for adults and several poetry books for children.

M.S. Reagan currently lives in Roanoke, Virginia, while she pursues her MFA at Hollins University.

Laura Schaffer is a Virginia-born poet whose work has been accepted in *3Elements Review* and *The Blue Mountain Review*. She has an MA in Appalachian Studies from Appalachian State University and a forthcoming MFA from Boston University.

Kim Shegog has an MFA from Converse College and an MA in English from The College of Charleston. She served as editor for *ReThinking the Notion of Waccamaw Indians* (2011). Her work has appeared in the *OWL*. She has taught creative writing and composition courses at Coastal Carolina University. She grew up in southwest Virginia and lives in Ohio.

Larry D. Thacker's poetry can be found in over a hundred publications including *Still: The Journal, Valparaiso Poetry Review, American Journal of Poetry, Poetry South, The Southern Poetry Anthology,* and *Appalachian Heritage*. His books include *Mountain Mysteries,* and the poetry books, *Drifting in Awe, Voice Hunting, Memory Train,* and the forthcoming *Feasts of Evasion and Grave Robber Confessional*. He holds an MFA from West Virginia Wesleyan College.

Ian C. Williams is pursuing an MFA at Oklahoma State University, and edits the online poetry magazine, *JARFLY*. His poems have appeared or are forthcoming in *Crab Orchard Review, The New Territory,* and *Blue Earth Review*, among others, and his chapbook, *House of Bones,* is available from the National Federation of State Poetry Societies. He grew up in Fairmont, West Virginia, and now lives with his wife, Bailey, along with their two dogs and two cats.

Jeff Worley is the current Poet Laureate of Kentucky. He has published six books, four chapbooks, and edited a poetry anthology, titled *What Comes Down to Us* (University Press of Kentucky, 2009). Worley's poems have also appeared widely in magazines in the United States and Canada for the past forty-five years, and he is the recipient of numerous awards and honors.

Marianne Worthington is co-founder and poetry editor of *Still: The Journal*. She is author of the chapbook *Larger Bodies Than Mine*, winner of the 2007 Appalachian Book of the Year Award. Her work has appeared in *Grist, Shenandoah, Appalachian Heritage, 94 Creations, Pine Mountain Sand & Gravel, Kudzu*, and many other publications. She lives, writes, and teaches in southeastern Kentucky.

www.ingramcontent.com/pod-product-compliance
Lightning Source LLC
Chambersburg PA
CBHW070603180626
46817CB00005B/1980